D0248047

Developing quality RE

Wouldn't it be good...?

... **if** pupils and parents were pleasantly surprised by their first experiences of RE, setting aside negative views of the subject, and finding it imaginative, engaging, creative, challenging and relevant?

... **if** it was one of their favourite lessons, so that when they knew an RE lesson was coming up they asked, 'What will we do this time, Sir?'

... **if** work in RE was making a special contribution to their skills in language, self-expression, co-operation and understanding?

... **if** RE was enabling them to develop attitudes of confidence and thoughtfulness about their own beliefs, and tolerance and respect towards other people?

... **if** children found space in RE to explore their own beliefs, and to spend time building up understanding of different world religions?

... **if** they had the chance to think about their own experiences of life, in the light of some of the treasures of faith?

... **if** they found in their RE ways to respond to the experiences of life, both happy and sad, that helped them to be more fully human?

... **if** Ofsted inspectors noticed that RE was making a significant contribution to the whole school's aims, and to the spiritual and moral development of all pupils?

... **if** at the end of their time at your school children made the kind of comments quoted above right?

'RE gave me the chance to ask the questions that had always puzzled me about God.'

•

'I really enjoyed learning not just about Christianity (my own religion) but other religions. Living in a multicultural society, it's important to understand what goes on around you. I think RE definitely makes you a more thoughtful person.'

•

'I have been given an insight into many other cultures and beliefs. The most satisfying aspect is that RE is helping me to mature in my attitude to life. RE enables me to develop my own concepts and views, and it's a mind-expanding experience.'

•

'I have found it good to learn from religions about how believers cope with everyday life.'

These comments come from pupils at the end of their RE courses, but quality RE begins with the very early years. **This book aims to provide teachers with information and practical ideas that will enable them to plan more effective, inspiring and challenging RE across the 4–19 age-range.**

RE can be a difficult subject to teach because it deals with truth claims in an uncertain field and its area of enquiry is vast. Some teachers are uncertain about the contribution RE can make to pupils' learning, and others find it a hard subject to teach because of their own experience of religion and life. Those with strong religious convictions of their own need to find an educational approach to RE; the same applies to the teacher who is an atheist or an agnostic. Pupils often come to RE with negative attitudes, picked up from a secular society in which religion can be marginalised, and parents sometimes may question the aims which a school is pursuing.

These problems should not obscure the rich potential of the subject to contribute to the human development of young people. High quality Religious Education can draw upon some of the great religions of the world and enable pupils to explore the questions of meaning that life throws up in the light of the insights of faith. RE can also enable young people to carry forward their own personal search for what is true, and what is good. **We hope this book will enable teachers who use it to build this kind of RE.**

A model for quality RE

Life Questions

Questions of authority
Who can I trust?

•

Questions of origins
How did I get here?

•

Questions of identity
Who is the 'real' me?

•

Questions of destiny
Where am I going?

•

Questions of purpose
What is it all for?

•

Questions of morality
How do I know
what is right?

•

Questions of value
What matters most?

•

Questions of meaning
Do I have any
significance?

What does it mean to be human?

This is the fundamental question which should underpin the whole process of education. There are many dimensions to our humanity but, perhaps above all, being human is about seeking significance, asking questions about meaning and purpose.

It is here that we find ourselves in the realm of Religious Education.

Shared human experience

The religious quest begins with those experiences or encounters common to all human beings which raise questions of meaning: encounter with oneself, with others on the level of personal relationships, with others in the wider sense of an engagement with our society and our culture and ultimately with the whole human race, and with the natural world.

It is these encounters which provoke a variety of conflicting emotions and which are the raw materials of the religious quest.

Personal search

Though many of these 'raw materials' are common, the search for meaning is a personal one. We all seek our own answers to questions such as those shown on the left.

World faiths

It is not necessary to be a 'religious' person in the conventional sense of the term to reflect on shared human experience and to engage in personal search. Nor is it the sole preserve of RE or RME within the curriculum.

RE has a distinct, and distinctive, contribution to make, however, in directing pupils' attention to the major world faiths as a rich source of insights into these issues.

Quality RE

The key to quality RE lies in our ability to relate these three 'fields' of enquiry – shared human experience, personal search and the insights of world faiths – to one another.

Reflection on shared human experience and personal search can, and should, occur throughout the curriculum.

It is the attempt to relate these to the insights of world faiths that makes RE *religious* education.

Overview: What's the job of the subject leader?

A pivotal role

The role of the subject leader is a pivotal one in both primary and secondary schools. The following pages of this handbook seek to develop some of the key areas which any subject leader needs to be aware of and to plan to develop. Further guidance can be found in three publications which address specifically the role of subject leader.

National Standards for Subject Leaders (1998)

In this document the Teacher Training Agency (TTA) outlined the nature of the role of the subject leader. **It identified five areas:**

- core purpose of the subject leader;
- key outcomes of subject leadership;
- professional knowledge and understanding;
- skills and attributes;
- key areas of subject leadership.

Effective Subject Leadership in RE (1999)

The Association of RE Inspectors, Advisers and Consultants (AREIAC) produced a subject-specific (RE) version of the TTA's guidelines which also included a useful needs analysis and target-setting grid.

Good teaching, effective departments (2002)

Ofsted published the findings of an HMI survey of subject teaching in secondary schools completed in 2000/2001. **The report identified five areas** in which schools which were effective overall performed significantly better than the national average:

- the quality of leadership and management;
- the quality of the monitoring of teaching;
- the quality and the range of learning opportunities;
- the breadth and balance of the curriculum;
- the quality of monitoring of pupils' performance.

Effective subject leadership in RE results in pupils who are enthusiastic about RE and regard the subject as being of interest and relevance, and through the key attitudes of respect, open mindedness, curiosity and self esteem contribute to a reflective and supportive learning environment.
Standards for Subject Leaders in RE *(AREIAC, PCfRE, CULRE and the TTA, 1999)*

Core purpose of the subject leader:

- **provides professional leadership** for the subject to secure high quality teaching, effective use of resources and improved standards of learning and achievement for all pupils;

- **provides leadership and direction for the subject and ensures it is managed and organised to meet the aims and objectives of the school and the subject.** While the head teacher and governors carry overall responsibility for school improvement, a subject leader has responsibility for securing high standards of teaching and learning in their subject as well as playing a major role in the development of school policy and practice. Throughout their work, a subject leader ensures that practices improve the quality of education provided, meet the needs and aspirations of all pupils, and raise standards of achievement in the school;

- **plays a key role in supporting, guiding and motivating teachers of the subject, and other adults.** Subject leaders evaluate the effectiveness of teaching and learning, the subject curriculum and progress towards targets for pupils and staff to inform future priorities and targets for the subject;

- **identifies needs in their own subject and recognises that these must be considered in relation to the overall needs of the school.** It is important that a subject leader has an understanding of how their subject contributes to school priorities and to the overall education and achievement of all pupils.

Source: National Standards for Subject Leaders, TTA (1998)

Law and RE

Does this concern me?

RE takes place within a framework of legislation and guidance[1]. It is important not to confuse the two.

The **legislation** is contained in a number of different Parliamentary Acts (the Education Act of 1998 reinforced the Education Acts of 1944, 1988 and 1992). These form the statutory basis for the planning and delivery of RE in our schools.

Non-statutory guidance comes in different forms: for example, Circular 1/94 (DfES), Schemes of work for RE and Non-statutory guidance for RE (QCA), Guidance on inspecting subjects – primary and secondary (Ofsted).

What does legislation on RE require?

1 RE is to be delivered for all registered pupils on the school roll (including those in reception classes and in the sixth form), unless they have been withdrawn for whole or part of the RE curriculum by their parent(s).[2]

2 In community, voluntary controlled[3] and foundation schools (religious and non-religious), RE is to be delivered in accordance with the Locally Agreed Syllabus for Religious Education. In voluntary aided[4] schools, RE is to be delivered in accordance with the school's trust deeds, which generally means following their faith community guidelines.

3 Agreed syllabuses vary in presentation, style and content. They all have to ensure that RE content focuses predominantly on Christianity whilst taking account of the other principal religious traditions represented in Great Britain[5]. Two aspects of RE common to most agreed syllabuses are: learning about religions and learning from religion. Most are drawn up on the assumption that RE will occupy about 5% of curriculum time (roughly one hour per week).[6]

What are the implications at school level?

You must be familiar with and use the correct syllabus for your type of school. Knowing legislation can 'strengthen your hand' when you feel that RE is not being taken seriously enough.

The law in England and Wales makes provision for all pupils in community schools to receive a religious education that has been agreed between different religious communities, the LEA and the teachers. This legal framework has enabled us to develop over many years RE which makes it possible for all pupils to know their own roots and to respect the roots of others. These respectful possibilities are the envy of the world in some ways, as the steady stream of visitors from other countries to look at our RE shows.

[1] The legal framework varies between England, Wales, Northern Ireland and Scotland. What is presented here is basic information about England.

[2] The right of withdrawal was enshrined in law in the 1944 Education Act. It applies to schools of all types, even those with a religious foundation (aided or controlled). Teachers also have the right to withdraw from teaching RE.

[3] In voluntary controlled schools, parents can request that RE is delivered in accordance with the trust deeds of the school rather than with the Locally Agreed Syllabus.

[4] In voluntary aided schools, parents can request that RE is delivered in accordance with the Locally Agreed Syllabus rather than with the school's trust deeds, if there is no school that would be delivering the Locally Agreed Syllabus which they could reasonably be expected to send their child(ren) to.

[5] Usually: Buddhism, Hinduism, Islam, Judaism and Sikhism.

[6] Dearing Report. Many agreed syllabuses have been drawn up on the expectation of 5% curriculum time for pupils in Key Stages 1 to 4. The report suggests that if a school is giving significantly less time than this to RE it cannot be meeting children's entitlement in RE.

Planning RE and policy

Planning a scheme of work for RE

Planning is vital. Investing precious time in planning has many benefits for teachers and pupils:

- It frees you to become a more effective teacher.

- It relieves stress and pressure, enabling quality teaching and learning to take place.

- It is a shared process, drawing upon the expertise and insights of everyone involved, giving a sense of ownership and encouraging enthusiasm and team work.

There are three key steps in planning the teaching and learning activities pupils will undertake in the classroom:

- long-term planning (key stage overview);

- medium-term planning (units of work);

- short-term planning (lessons).

This section of the *Handbook* will give you a clear outline of the process needed, with key points to consider and develop.

Long-term planning: the key stage overview

Whose responsibility?   Subject leader, RE co-ordinator or Head of Department.

What does it involve?   Organising the programmes of study across the phases or key stage(s) to ensure syllabus or specification requirements are met.

Important to remember: Planning should ensure continuity and progression both within and between phases or key stages of pupils' learning.

Medium-term planning: planning units of work

Whose responsibility?   Subject leader, RE co-ordinator or Head of Department in consultation with class teachers.

What does it involve?   Detailed planning of how each required element or study unit is to be delivered to meet the required attainment targets and learning outcomes.

Important to remember: Planning provides a clear sequence of activities to promote progression and includes a range of teaching and learning strategies to encourage pupil participation and skill development.

Short-term planning: lesson planning

Whose responsibility?   Class teacher.

What does it involve?   Clear planning of what exactly will be done in the lesson to enable the intended learning outcomes to be achieved, taking account of the different needs of pupils.

Important to remember: Develop a range of teaching and learning strategies to encourage pupil participation and skill development.

Three levels of curriculum planning: some points to consider

Long-term planning is necessary to:

- **meet** statutory requirements (for example, LEA Agreed Syllabus, Scottish RME 5–14);

- **select** (if appropriate) which principal religions in addition to Christianity are to be taught in each year;

- **decide** whether RE is to be taught by themes, religions or both;

- **check** that if RE is taught in themes, all RE attainment targets will be met;

- **organise** how the programmes of study will be divided up across the years;

- **consider** how much time will be needed for each programme of study;

- **plan** for continuity and progression within a pupil's time at the school;

- **audit** existing resources against the scheme of work, determine deficiencies and make provision for resource development for RE;

- **consider** staff development needs.

Medium-term planning is necessary to determine:

- **key teaching issues:** the key topics or questions you want to develop, taken from the programme of study. It is good practice to formulate teaching units around questions (as in the QCA schemes of work for RE in England) as this is an effective means of helping teachers and pupils keep a clear focus and make better progress;

- **intended learning outcomes:** what pupils will know, understand and be able to do as a result of completing the unit;

- **the range and sequence of teaching and learning activities:** bearing in mind that pupils learn best in a variety of ways and that effective learning comes from using a variety of strategies matched to the intended learning outcomes;

- **assessment opportunities:** keeping in mind level descriptions or end-of-key-stage statements of attainment where appropriate and the need to assess a variety of competences using a range of assessment methods including self-assessment.

Short-term planning produces quality RE when:

- **you are clear about what you are aiming to achieve:** intended learning outcomes in terms of knowledge, understanding, skills, attitudes;

- **you are able to use this understanding to assess** how well pupils achieve and use this to inform your future lesson planning;

- **you are confident about all aspects of the lesson:** factual content, activity instructions, activities to support pupils with special needs, organisation of resources;

- **you are able to utilise** current events, active learning strategies, choice and humour to engage the pupils in their learning.

School policy statement

Religious Education needs a policy statement which accurately describes the actual practice in RE and which also:

- sets out clearly the rationale, aims and objectives;
- provides all teachers with a framework;
- informs parents and inspectors about the RE curriculum within the school.

Many schools will have a standard framework for curriculum policy statements.

To adapt such a framework to meet the requirements of RE, the following should be included:

1 Legal requirements and time allocation for Religious Education:
- making it clear that RE is distinct from collective worship, which is not counted as curriculum time.

2 Statement about the place of RE in the curriculum:
- an important opportunity to explain the valuable contribution RE makes to pupils' development and to help colleagues understand what RE is and is not!

3 Aims of RE:
- based on the syllabus (for example, LEA Agreed Syllabus) but indicating school priorities.

4 Attainment targets:
- taken from syllabus documents but explained in a way which helps understanding.

5 Content and approach:
- religions taught;
- approach to teaching religions: thematic, by religion or a mixture of both.

6 Scheme of work outline:
- an overview of teaching units for each phase or key stage.

7 Methodology:
- how RE is taught. Outline of teaching and learning strategies encouraged and used.
- reference to the development of skills and attitudes.

8 Resources:
- books, artefacts, video, ICT hardware and software, local resource centre address, local contacts.

9 Assessment:
- a brief statement summarising how the school makes use of intended learning outcomes, levels or end-of-key-stage statements to recognise and report on pupils' progress in RE.

10 RE and other aspects of the curriculum:
- **Spiritual, moral, social and cultural development of pupils:** a statement of the specific contribution RE makes to pupils' development in these areas.
- **Inclusion:** a sentence summarising the school's commitment to valuing the opinions, beliefs and practices of all, and handling minority groups and opinions with sensitivity. A statement about provision for pupils in RE with a range of needs including those with special education needs and those who are gifted or talented in the subject.

11 Withdrawal:
- a statement of the rights of parents to withdraw their children from RE, expressed in a way which demonstrates the school's positive attitude towards RE and the benefits it brings to pupils.

12 Further references:
- Syllabus (for example, LEA Agreed Syllabus, examination specifications, Trust Deed);
- RE subject leader job description.

Target-setting

How can we measure, raise and manage pupils' performance in RE?

Many schools and RE subject leaders are involved in attempts to measure improvements in pupils' performance, target-setting and value-added measures of attainment.

Some of those involved in this process would argue that RE requires a special category, as there are aspects of RE which are not covered by an assessment scale, whether that scale be the one provided by the syllabus (such as the LEA Agreed Syllabus) or the QCA's non-statutory guidelines for RE.

How does an assessment scale affect target-setting?

Formal assessment scales attempt to provide a useful set of criteria, against which to make judgements with integrity and rigour, and with which realistic targets can be set both for the subject and for individual pupils.

In order to develop useful subject target-setting, it is essential to have systems of comparison: for example, between phases, between subjects and internally. Data such as this will provide some of the information needed to evaluate the target-setting process.

This, combined with general data available to the school, will provide information which will advise judgements made in RE.

Should all aspects of RE be assessed?

It is obviously not appropriate to measure or quantify those aspects of RE which involve the spiritual development of pupils. However, schools are required to provide a wide range of opportunities for spiritual development across the curriculum, including RE, and it would be expected that the life of the school as a community would be affected as an outcome of this provision.

This, therefore, results in two categories of target-setting:

* **departmental**;

* **whole-school.**

> *If you keep a broad and open view of what assessment is, and grapple with the issues, if you follow a few basic guidelines and if you are both systematic and flexible in your practical approach to assessment, you will quickly find that it pays dividends for the pupils as learners and for yourself as a teacher.*
>
> *John Rudge*

A Process Targets

* **Entitlement targets**
  These will aim for agreed minimum entitlements for all pupils, such as:
  * appropriate time given for RF;
  * being taught by a subject specialist;
  * opportunities to be involved in visits and receive visitors;
  * access to valid resources, including ICT;
  * opportunities to follow an accredited course at 14+ and 16+.

* **Support targets**
  These will aim for agreed levels of support for the department and its work, for example from:
  * governors;
  * Senior Management Team;
  * faculty structures;
  * parents;
  * whole-school programmes and initiatives.

* **Enrichment targets**
  These will aim for the kind of RE that includes special opportunities for any pupil to engage more profoundly with the RE agenda, for example through:
  * celebratory events;
  * charitable activity;
  * inter-school work;
  * ICT innovations;
  * community of enquiry for the most able;
  * expressive arts opportunities for spiritual development.

How can RE contribute to whole-school targets?

Apart from the subject's contribution to the development of literacy and numeracy, there are some key contributions to the development of creative thinking skills and emotional and spiritual literacy.

Arguably, more than any other part of the curriculum, RE gives teachers scope to value pupils' opinions, to increase pupils' self-esteem and to encourage them to question their own beliefs and values.

How can departmental targets help to raise standards?

Realistic, but nevertheless challenging, targets will help to provide a strategic planning focus.

The list of **Process Targets** and **Product Targets** outlined in these pages suggests a broader approach to target-setting.

Some key evaluation questions:

- How do we know how successfully the department targets are being met?

- Are they realistic and sufficiently challenging?

- Do they meet the needs of individual pupils, particularly enabling all pupils to have access to tasks, whilst providing scope for higher attainers?

- Is the quality of learning being affected by the use of target-setting?

- Are pupils involved in the evaluation process?

What are the wider implications for RE?

- Some questions that would need to be addressed by the subject leader involve issues around performance management, due to the nature of RE, and the fact that there will be many occasions when it is not appropriate to record achievement (for example, within the QCA's second attainment target, 'learning from religion').

- How does the school address the fact that not all pupils progress through the levels, in the same way that might be expected in other subjects? For example, creative and emotional responses to a particular unit of work might result in a unique outcome, not in line with the projected target.

Target-setting and vision

Regular evaluation will indicate the short-term effectiveness of target-setting within RE. However, the long-term impact on pupils' lives is incalculable, and the school can only hope that individuals will be introduced to a journey of self-discovery, expression and fulfilment.

B Product Targets

- **Performance targets**
  These will aim for measurable, externally validated, statistical measures of pupil attainment and performance in RE courses, for example:
  - GCSE, Standard Grade, Highers and AS or A2 level grades;
  - any value-added measures (though these are not easily available in RE).

- **Other output targets**
  These will be used to measure individual performance in the teaching of RE, possibly internally constructed, possibly not easily open to outside or statistical measures, for example:
  - take-up of accredited courses;
  - application of a scale (such as the QCA's non-statutory eight-level scale) to entry and end-of-key-stage tests;
  - pupils' self-evaluation and evaluation of the 'RE experience'.

For target setting to be effective it needs to be undertaken in a climate which actively maintains and enhances pupils' self-esteem.

Warwickshire County Council, Guidance for teachers

Learning strategies and challenging tasks

Expectations

Standards in RE have been criticised for being low. A variety of reasons can be suggested, including: lack of specialist teachers, little support for the subject from head teachers and governors, insufficient time on the timetable, lack of continuity in the team delivering the subject, pressure on time from other areas of the curriculum, little opportunity for subject-specific INSET, low morale among staff.

Where standards and teacher expectation are low, an evaluation of the types of tasks set and positive action on any findings will help reverse the trend. The evaluation should be done against a background of the assessment model for the subject provided by the syllabus, and that of the school. These pages provide a starting point.

Teachers

Raising expectations can be a challenge for the RE teacher. It may mean:

- **evaluating** teaching methods, resources and tasks set. Is RE challenging all pupils?

- **comparing** standards with those in another school, or with reference to the QCA's non-statutory eight-level scale as a benchmark. Does the subject match up to history, or to level 5?

- **ensuring** that the classroom culture is one of praise, encouragement and support. Can pupils take pride in RE?

- **allowing** pupils to take more control of their learning, to make mistakes and learn from them in a supportive environment. Do pupils choose their own learning paths and styles in RE?

Pupils

For the pupil, being set more challenging tasks will mean:

- **increased** sense of achievement in RE, boosting self-esteem;

- **expectations** of a more independent approach to learning, perhaps following up their own 'big questions' for themselves;

- **opportunities** to develop new or existing skills, in reflection or spiritual insight;

- **increased** awareness of what is expected of them in RE;

- **potential** for greater enjoyment of the religious enquiry, less disaffection;

- **opportunity** for exam success, where RS is an option.

> *In order to improve further standards in primary RE, schools should increase the challenge of tasks by asking pupils to interpret, analyse, evaluate and reflect on what they learn rather than simply write descriptively, reiterate stories or record pictorially; training pupils to listen to, analyse and evaluate what others say in discussion, making their own contribution informed and thoughtful.*
>
> Standards in Primary RE, *Ofsted, 1998*

> *The most common contributor to low standards in RE is low expectations seen in written tasks which lack challenge ... the quality of discussion and tasks set for pupils are generally satisfactory at best and often poor.*
>
> *Tasks requiring extended writing on the whole require no more than descriptive writing based heavily on text book accounts ... but in many schools even this type of extended writing takes second place to a regular diet of completing sentences, pointless drawing and short comprehension answers to questions.*
>
> *These findings apply to specialists and non-specialists alike.*
>
> Key Stage 3 RE, *Barbara Wintersgill, HMI for RE, 2000*

Guidelines for setting challenging tasks

Based on Bloom's Taxonomy of educational objectives (1956), the following table is designed to provide a prompt for setting challenging tasks. A task is more likely to be challenging if one of the prompt words (or equivalent) shown alongside the high order skills is used.

Skill	Order	Prompt	Example from RE
SYNTHESIS (Create)	**High**	Create Compose Invent Hypothesise What would happen if? Design Be original Combine from several sources	**Primary:** Design your ideal world. How would it be different from today and why? **Secondary:** How do you think Christian belief and practice would be different if Jesus had not died on the cross?
EVALUATION (Judge)	**High**	Give an opinion Judge Rate – for example, best/worst Choose Recommend What to do differently?	**Primary:** Which rules (from any faith and/or secular) are the most important and why? **Secondary:** Choose one of the Sikh Gurus and say why you think his contribution to the development of Sikhism was significant.
ANALYSIS (Relationships)	**High**	Categorise Compare/contrast Alike/different Cause and effect Relevant/irrelevant Find fallacies Fact/opinion	**Primary:** Compare the accounts of Jesus' birth in the gospels. **Secondary:** How and why is a mosque different from a church?
APPLICATION (Use)	**Middle**	Use what you have learned in another situation	**Primary:** What do you learn about forgiveness from the story of Zacchaeus? **Secondary:** Use what you have learned about forgiveness and set it in the context of a modern day situation (for example, role-play).
KNOWLEDGE COMPREHENSION	**Low**	Tell Find Summarise Locate Name	**Primary:** Summarise what happened to Moses when he was a baby. **Secondary:** Name the Four Noble Truths.

Team-building for better RE: teachers with other specialisms

A major challenge for the subject co-ordinator in the primary schools of today is that of enabling colleagues with other specialisms and priorities to do a good job efficiently, with enthusiasm and integrity. Similarly, in secondary schools, the head of RE often leads a team of colleagues with other specialisms. In RE, perhaps more than in other subjects, this can be compounded by the different approaches to the subject among a staff team.

Some teachers have a great commitment to and interest in teaching their own faith, but not other faiths. Some teachers question the place of RE in the curriculum, often because they misunderstand the educational rationale for the subject, sometimes because they felt indoctrinated through their own experience of RE. Some teachers may exercise their right to opt out of RE teaching on conscientious grounds.

In every case, the priorities of teachers are so many that RE will not be top of the list often or for long. This is quite reasonable, and it means that when the subject is considered, once a term at a staff meeting, or through an annual INSET session, the quality of input needs to be good, and the agenda needs to move forward, rather than chewing over old questions (for example, indoctrination).

The issue of confidence is perhaps the most crucial. Many excellent teachers, who are able, with a little work, to do their RE really well, feel so lacking in confidence in a subject where many different religions offer different solutions to life's uncertain riddles that their RE work is confined to telling stories, 'doing' festivals or discussing vaguely ethical stories from the newspapers. Team leaders need to find ways of building the confidence of colleagues so that more imaginative teaching and learning strategies can be developed. Such confidence grows where people can find a little time and space to share their concerns and to have them addressed. Would it help to devote a teacher day to RE?

Strategies to build up successful RE teams – are all these happening in your school?

The subject co-ordinator needs to develop **strategies** such as the following to build up the staff team's understanding of RE, and their confidence to deliver the subject well:

- **ways of addressing** people's reasonable concerns about aims in RE;

- a clearly structured **policy statement**, devised by all those involved, and widely understood (see page 7);

- **schemes of work** that are easy to use, practical and comprehensive;

- **team planning** that involves everybody from the start – though the subject leader will provide most of the ideas;

- well thought out and **varied resources**, stored in usable ways;

- **support** for teachers where they lack confidence (conversation, teacher observation, books to refer to, access to training and other kinds of support);

- **clarity about the outcomes** of RE work by pupils in different age-groups. Examples of a range of pupils' achievements and clear reference to the assessment structures of your syllabus, or to the national eight-level scale of achievements;

- **agreement about the time** which is spent on RE in the classroom;

- **monitoring of pupils' work** in RE (to avoid 'ten in the bed' syndrome, where one subject 'falls out', and it's always RE!).

TWOS in RE

A PCfRE project to assist Teachers with Other Specialisms (TWOS) in their RE work was undertaken from 1997 to 2000 as part of the RE and School Effectiveness project at Brunel University's BFSS National RE Centre. Among the findings of the project, there was much of practical significance for any subject leader in RE, including the following ideas:

- RE is more often taught by TWOS than almost any other subject (exceptions might be only ICT and Citizenship).

- While this is not an ideal situation, many TWOS bring their gifts as teachers to the subject, including expertise in particular parts of the RE field. (Historians may be good at teaching interpretation, drama teachers at engaging pupils with issues, science teachers in tackling empirical approaches to religion.)

- The first need for TWOS is to find and assimilate a professional rationale for their RE work. This won't happen without training and time to think about what the subject is for.

- RE should not be taught by the unwilling or the press-ganged. This is unfair on teachers and pupils and is unprofessional.

- RE teaching deserves to be planned on the same basis as teaching other subjects. If there is a long-term need to use staff without training, then failing a new appointment of a specialist teacher, the minimum satisfactory approach involves continuity of deployment, and appropriate professional development for those involved.

Questions for RE team leaders:

- In what ways have you been successful in building your RE team? What factors have enabled this success?

- What are the most difficult aspects of building a team for RE teaching in your school? Who can you talk to about addressing these problems?

- What do you see as the next steps forward in building more successful RE across the team? How can these be monitored?

Using TWOS can be successful, but can also contribute to low standards. Careful and supportive monitoring and intervention to change and improve the quality of teaching is the key to success.

What do you like about teaching RE?

Listening to the class argue about things that matter, instead of who's got better eye shadow.

One respondent to the TWOS questionnaire

In spite of the continued nervousness with RE of some teachers, no [primary] school inspected had considered using teachers with specialist expertise to teach classes other than their own. As a result, many pupils were not receiving the best teaching the school could offer.

Ofsted judgement

Teachers with other specialisms are commonly used in RE in both primary and secondary schools.

Such teachers can do their RE work very well, but they deserve three kinds of support as a minimum: the leadership of a specialist, the time for training and meeting and planning with the subject leader and continuity of deployment from year to year.

Given even these basic supports, TWOS can make a good contribution to RE.

Without them, poor teaching is all too likely.

The PCfRE 'TWOS' project

Inclusion issues for professionals: matching work to pupils' needs

Inclusion is about equal opportunities for all pupils, whatever their age, gender, ethnicity, attainment, background. It pays particular attention to the provision made for, and the achievement of, different groups within a school. **These groups include:**

- girls and boys;
- faith groups;
- minority ethnic groups, travellers, asylum seekers and refugees;
- pupils who need support to learn English as a foreign language;
- lower achieving pupils;
- gifted and talented pupils;
- children 'looked after' by the local authority;
- other children such as sick children, young carers, those from families under stress, pregnant school-girls, teenage mothers;
- any pupils who are at risk of disaffection and exclusion.

Source: Evaluating Educational Inclusion, *Ofsted, 2001*

A broad and balanced curriculum

The statutory inclusion statement declares that schools have a responsibility to provide a broad and balanced curriculum which meets the specific needs of all pupils. It sets out **three principles** for developing a more inclusive curriculum:

- setting suitable learning challenges;
- responding to pupils' diverse learning needs;
- overcoming potential barriers to learning and assessment for all pupils.

Inspection

Inspectors (Ofsted) are asked to report on:

'How well the teaching meets the needs of all the pupils.'

They look at:

'the extent to which teachers use methods which enable all pupils to learn effectively.'

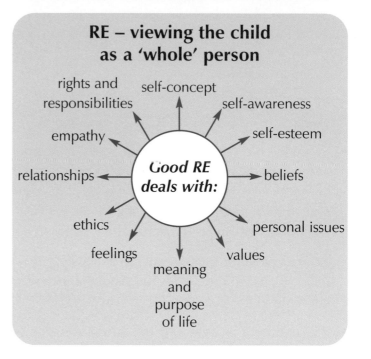

RE – viewing the child as a 'whole' person

Good RE deals with: self-concept, self-awareness, self-esteem, beliefs, personal issues, values, meaning and purpose of life, feelings, ethics, relationships, empathy, rights and responsibilities

Developing an all-inclusive classroom environment in RE

It can be difficult for the teacher to make a judgement of a pupil's level of need, self-esteem, 'intelligence' or preferred learning style. The information in this section will provide some tools to assess the needs of individual pupils and indicate steps needed to adjust expectations and experiment with other teaching and learning activities which may be more appropriate.

The importance of self-esteem

It is well known that self-esteem affects the way we think, our motivation and our behaviour. In the classroom, the teacher can play an important role in increasing the self-esteem of pupils by creating an appropriate and positive learning environment. **This includes the teacher's own attitudes, behaviour and teaching style as well as the learning opportunities they provide.**

> *To steal a person's struggle is to steal their self esteem.*
> *Psychologist*

Gender and achievement in RE

Teacher research into RE revealed that boys:

- liked discussing moral issues which drew on their own experiences and viewpoint;

- felt there was too much emphasis on neat and 'pretty' presentation of work;

- wanted activities like role-play, discussion of philosophical issues, access to ICT, visual work, games, and humour.

Source: Underachieving boys and undervalued girls?,
AREIAC, 2002

The provision of fair and balanced opportunities for both boys and girls is a matter of justice. But perhaps paying attention to boys' needs will help RE teachers to provide effectively for both genders.

Meeting the needs of boys (and girls) through attending to:

- the wider use of short, focused RE tasks;

- setting more short-term achievable goals;

- being explicit about expectations;

- using levels of attainment (to give a 'fix' on expected standards);

- giving regular feedback (for example, at the end of a lesson by asking what has been learned);

- using praise more;

- using humour more;

- focusing on problem-solving or problem-centred activities;

- turning discussion lessons into 'argument' lessons;

- using more practical activities and movement – for example, drama, role-play, games, simulations;

- using video in combination with challenging questions;

- using ICT more often;

- developing more imaginative approaches to assessing achievement, so not so much focus on writing only;

- using thinking skills strategies;

- focusing on moral dilemmas (for example, the ethics of sport);

- developing a wider range of homework approaches, such as tabulating survey results and writing conclusions;

- using writing frames;

- using RE 'detective stories' and science fiction;

- managing group work more effectively, planning for different combinations (for example, mixed gender seating and paired work).

Special Educational Needs in RE

The spectrum of special needs is particularly broad and teachers need to plan their RE accordingly. Using sensory active learning strategies can help all pupils to learn but particularly those identified as having some kind of learning difficulty.

More detailed guidance for addressing the needs of those with learning difficulties can be found in QCA's document *Planning, teaching and assessing the curriculum for pupils with learning difficulties – RE* (QCA/01/750). This includes level descriptors for those working below level one.

What do lower ability pupils need in RE?

The needs are similar to the needs of all pupils:

- to have their entitlements for RE met;

- to be able to make progress from where they are, to their own 'next steps' on learning about religion and learning from religion;

- to progress with regard to their own abilities, not to be held back by particular learning impairments, for example in writing or in reading;

- small steps forward, one at a time – targets broken down into small achievable progress points;

- to experience achievement, not just failure;

- to be encouraged and praised whenever appropriate;

- to see the importance, value, relevance of their own learning;

- to benefit from the range of learning styles on offer, not just doing 'question one' (the information-gathering bit);

- to have the opportunity to take up chances for spiritual, moral or cultural development.

Strategies to increase learning potential

In the table below, some general strategies are given for increasing the learning potential of RE for lower achieving pupils, along with an example of each. Teachers might consider together whether these examples fit their needs, and add eight more which relate to other age-groups.

Strategy for SEN pupils	Examples from RE classrooms
Multi-sensory approaches (see, touch, taste, smell, hear, feel).	A small group of SEN pupils in a class of 6–7-year-olds arranged a 'feel, smell, taste' activity for the whole class with a classroom assistant, using some of the special foods of Divali and Easter. They recorded responses from the class on a tick sheet for a discussion about 'celebrating with food'.
Provide raw material, rather than asking pupils to find or generate it themselves; reduce research to make time for thinking, analysis, reflection.	While most of a class of 8–9 year olds researched 'Christmas around the world' from a book box and other sources, three lower achieving pupils were asked to compare six African Christmas cards with the story of Jesus from St Matthew's gospel, and find differences between them to report to the whole class. A classroom assistant read with them.
Time. Working slowly is appropriate, and finding time is a good differentiation strategy for many pupils.	The teacher set a class of 9–10-year-olds a choice of tasks about four parables, asking most children to do three of the tasks set. She asked five pupils on the SEN register to choose just one task and she read just one parable to them. Given more time, their work was more careful and was completed.
Group work (mixed or similar needs, for challenge). Through paired and small group work, children can progress much more effectively than alone.	In one lesson on welcoming a new baby, the teacher paired higher achieving readers with lower achieving pupils, asking them to read and report on Hindu and Christian customs at birth. In the next lesson pupils planned a baby-welcoming ceremony for the 21st century. She worked closely with one group of five lower achieving pupils, leaving other groups to exercise initiative.
Support staff working with groups or individuals through carefully planned RE programmes targeted to need (for example, for symbolic understanding, or for considering reasons for holding a belief).	The teacher identified a group within a class of 11-year-olds who were less able than others to construct religious arguments. She used a lesson with a classroom assistant to get this group to complete writing frames about why some people believe there is no God. In the next lesson, all pupils were asked to complete writing frames about a different religious argument: what happens when we die?
Differentiated resources, such as textbooks, worksheets, tasks, assessments.	One teacher always sets three tasks on school-produced worksheets, which offer simpler or more complex starting points. Another uses two versions of the same textbook, one with a lower reading access level. A third teacher devises 'tiered' assessment tasks which cover four different levels, enabling all to show what they can do.
Skip over the research or information-gathering, and set the tasks focused on other skills such as application or reflection first.	In a class of 8–9-year-olds, lower achieving pupils were given a 'head start' sheet of information about Muslim and Jewish worship, and asked to respond to 'why do they do that?' questions in discussion and in writing. Most of the class began by researching worship from textbook sources.
Reduce the 'waste' of time on purposeless writing activity. Ask: 'How could they learn this without, or without much, writing?'	In a topic on expressing spirituality through art, SEN pupils from three parallel classes of 12-year-olds skipped two lessons of written work to begin designing and making stained glass designs based on the 'I am…' sayings of Jesus. They received a sheet of copied notes to make sure they could access the curriculum without writing, but concentrated their activity on spiritual expression in art.

Challenging the most able pupils

RE is centrally concerned with:

ultimate questions; critical thinking; analysis and interpretation; multifaceted phenomena and concepts; truth-seeking.

RE can provide the most able with opportunities to:

- develop and apply knowledge, understanding, skills and processes (such as critical thinking, interpretation, insight, reflection, synthesis);

- demonstrate high levels of understanding, insight, discernment, and mature reflective thinking;

- engage with story, symbol, metaphor, allegory and its approach to meaning-making;

- explore a range of approaches to philosophy;

- develop thinking skills such as argument, reasoning and logical analysis.

Source: Meeting the needs of gifted, talented and most able pupils in RE, QCA, 2000.

How can the needs of the most able be met?

- Set tasks which focus on skills such as the interpretation of symbol, metaphor, text or story.

- Use more demanding tasks and questions from key stages beyond the age of the pupil, to encourage use of analysis, argument, application of learning to new contexts.

- Set extension tasks which deepen understanding and reflection.

- Use a variety of questioning strategies to engage pupils' thinking at a deeper level.

- Use authentic material from inside the faiths (prayers, sacred texts, arguments, artefacts).

- Enable and encourage pupils to develop and use the correct terminology and language to discuss religious, spiritual, ethical and philosophical ideas.

- Use carefully planned self-assessment activities which help pupils identify their own learning needs.

- Develop target-setting strategies to encourage ambitious work.

How do I plan differentiated RE?

In planning for differentiation within a study unit or piece of work we need to:

- be aware of the strategies available;

- select carefully from these to achieve the learning objective with all pupils.

Strategies

There are many strategies for teaching and learning. Consider:

- auditing and listing the existing strategies used in the subject;

- drawing on strategies used in other curriculum areas;

- exploring the possibilities by trial and error;

- experimenting with and evaluating new methods.

Use a wide variety of learning strategies. Three main reasons for these are:

- the learning styles of pupils vary;

- a diet of the same type of work leads to boredom, distraction and inappropriate behaviour. A varied diet is more enjoyable and fun;

- teaching is more interesting – the monotony of delivering the same curriculum to a number of classes is diminished and the outcome more rewarding and stimulating.

Learning objectives

The key to any strategy's effectiveness is whether or not it results in the desired learning outcome.

The learning objective is crucial:

- it is the **teacher's guide** when planning and when assessing;

- it is the **pupil's goal** towards which he or she is working;

- it is the **pupil's marker** for his or her own achievement.

Differentiation

Differentiation takes account of pupil differences through the process of matching work, teaching styles and learning experiences to pupils' needs. This section provides suggestions to support developing an engaging RE curriculum through differentiation.

Some methods of differentiation to use in RE	
Method	**Example from RE**
Task: Whilst working on the same theme or topic, pupils tackle different tasks set by the teacher to match their individual abilities, needs and preferred learning style.	Pupils working on the theme of worship might be variously: • interviewing believers; • writing descriptions of mosques; • designing and making prayer mats; • commenting on the words of Islamic prayers.
Interest: Pupils are set a choice of tasks which offer different ways of achieving the same outcome. This enables them to develop an area of interest or use a particular skill such as artistic ability or ICT. Choice is the key.	In studying the ways religious beliefs are expressed in art, music and writing, pupils could choose one example, and write or record a review, or design a book or CD cover, to show their understanding of the religious meaning of the song, poem, painting. This is then presented to the rest of the group.
Resource: Independent learning and pupil responsibility can be enhanced by providing resources suitable for varied levels of ability and interest, and guiding pupils to work from appropriate books and other media.	Pupils are set a task requiring research – a wide range of different books, ICT and video resources is made available. Assessment criteria make it clear that an individual response showing thoughtful use of the resources will score highly.
Support: Differentiation by the level and type of support given by the teacher, peers and other staff. This may include: • breaking down the task into manageable steps (for example, use of a self-study guide); • offering extension; • monitoring to ensure pupils remain on task.	In an extended task on the Adam and Eve story, pupils experience a range of learning activities exploring art and animated versions of the story. They are set the task of producing an illustration of the meaning of the story for today, writing an explanation of their picture and completing an extension activity evaluating the story's lasting 'truth' for today. Levels statements outlining expected outcomes are shared with pupils from the start.
Ability: Grouping pupils in mixed- or selected-ability groups within a class may enable fullest participation and progress for all students. When such groupings are not desirable, the teacher can be prepared with reinforcement or extension tasks, or offer varying tasks with varying difficulty levels.	Pupils sort opinion statements to identify those they strongly agree or disagree with. Pupils sharing a similar point of view are grouped to work out reasons to support the viewpoint – the teacher can ensure either mixed-ability groups or higher/lower ability groups to support or extend pupils.
Outcome: This will always be differentiated when tasks are sufficiently challenging or open-ended – especially if they are supported by writing frames, sentence starters for discussion, extension questions, and so on.	Pupils asked to interpret and apply Gandhi's teaching on non-violence (*ahimsa*), and given support through writing frames and structured research activities, will elicit responses which range from a report on Gandhi's words and actions to an in-depth reflection and analysis of what the world would be like today if everyone put Gandhi's principles into practice.

Assessment, achievement and evaluation

Help needed!

Throughout the UK, the assessment of educational outcomes has been a growth industry in recent years, whether it is testing 7-year-olds, or pressing for 'higher still' achievements and standards. Often, the rush to the assessment try-line side-steps learning about religion, suggesting that RE is too spiritual to be assessed or (for some odd reason) bottom of the list for innovation.

Some syllabuses give helpful guidance. GCSEs and Standard Grade courses have led the way in assessing RS, and there is some published guidance from government agencies, but many schools and teachers continue to struggle with assessment in RE, and need further support. This is especially true for 5–14-year-old pupils.

In this section, we offer some practical classroom ideas for assessing achievements in Religious Education.

A broad definition of achievement

Achievements in RE cannot be easily measured in tick boxes or tally charts. Some teachers say that RE can't be assessed. If by this they mean to draw attention to RE's contribution to spiritual and moral development and the difficulty of finding instruments of assessment, or more particularly tests, that will assess empathy, moral development or spiritual insight, then a solid point is being made. But RE teachers can work effectively with the broadest possible definition of achievement.

Pupils have achieved something in RE if their thinking, creativity and skills are engaged, if their vision of truth, beauty and love has been stimulated. Something of value has occurred if pupils have taken part in conversation about beliefs and values that is secure, calm and thoughtful. They may also achieve a wider, deeper knowledge of religions and believers.

All this is achievement, and it is good to observe, monitor, celebrate, assess and record it.

Four uses of assessment

Formative assessment recognises when a child has achieved a target, acknowledges this positively, and plans future learning in the light of the achievement. So, when a child has shown that she has grasped the concept of 'worship' in Islam, the teacher may move on to give examples from different faiths, and diversify the learning. This is also known as 'assessment for learning'.

Summative assessment informs learners and others such as parents what has been achieved. In RE this means reporting to parents in line with the law, and sending information about progress to a new school on transfer. Results of external tests and published examinations are also examples of summative assessment.

Diagnostic assessment is intended to reveal weaknesses in knowledge or skills with a view to further development and putting things right. This may enable a teacher to decide that particular pupils lack a basic framework for understanding religion, or festival, or symbol, or belief. The remedy may lie in group work targeted to their needs or in discussion with individuals to build their conceptual framework. Good marking practice and self-assessment in RE are tools for diagnostic assessment.

Evaluative assessment seeks to measure the effectiveness of the teaching as a whole. Pupils' feedback on their RE is important here. Do they find it interesting? Are they learning a lot? A team who have taught the same material to different groups might compare the results and evaluate the course, and their own work. This evaluation is an important process if RE is to improve continuously.

National expectations in RE

The English Qualifications and Curriculum Authority (QCA) published in 2000 an eight-level scale of expectations for RE for the 5–14 age-range. The scale is non-statutory and offered as guidance only to agreed syllabus conferences, SACREs, LEAs and others. Many of the most recent Agreed Syllabuses are taking it up, and many more will follow suit in the next 5 years. Schools in Scotland and independent schools in England and Wales may also find that the issues raised by the potential of this scale are helpful.

According to the QCA scale the **key indicators of attainment** in RE are contained in three strands for attainment target 1 (learning about religions) and three strands for attainment target 2 (learning from religion).

Key indicators of attainment in RE (QCA)

Learning about religions

Knowledge and understanding of:

- religious beliefs and teachings;
- religious practices and lifestyles;
- ways of expressing meaning.

Learning from religion

Skills of asking and responding to:

- questions of identity and experience;
- questions of meaning and purpose;
- questions of values and commitments.

Expectations

Key stage 1

Levels 1-3, most achieving level 2 at EOKS 1, age 7.

Key stage 2

Levels 2-5, most achieving level 4 at EOKS 2, age 11.

Key stage 3

Levels 3-8, most achieving level 5/6 at EOKS 3, age 14.

Some observations: the eight-level scale

Integrity and choice

The scale will be of great importance to some teachers, but others will reject its use, and some will find it incompatible with their syllabuses. Professional integrity does not rest with one of these groups, but can be found in all of them. Many recent syllabuses are using the scale, or a version based upon it.

Breadth and balance

It is a good scale! The scale is skills-based, and does not prescribe content for RE. It balances 'learn about' and 'learn from' equally. It does not require an approach to assessment dominated by facts or by testing, but instead permits a range of broad approaches to gathering evidence of achievement. There are no perfect scales, though.

Ammunition and expectation

Clear criterion-referencing gives RE some ammunition in the 'status war'. It provides RE with a parallel structure to the subjects of the National Curriculum. Scales like this intend to establish expectations. By describing high standards, it may enable teachers and schools to aim more clearly for those standards. Does such a scale clarify expectations (for both teachers and pupils), and contribute to high standards? Well used, it can do. Teachers in practice quickly internalise such scales and use the levels as a piece of their professional toolkit. Experience in other subjects shows that RE professionals will easily develop a 'feel' for its use.

Validity and value

But do all such scales encourage box-ticking at the expense of validity? Do they undermine motivation for those who don't get the rewards of progress up the levels? Are they valid in assessing real, rich, deep, authentic learning, or only in pushing teaching towards specific and possibly impoverished objectives? These are idealistic and genuine questions, and can't be ignored. Many teachers can cite examples where achievement by pupils sometimes blows the scale out of the water. There are 7-year-olds whose RE fits best with a line or phrase from level 7. So the scale may judge the child, but never forget that the child may judge the scale too.

A national scale of expectations for RE (originally published by QCA)

Level 1
Pupils recount outlines of religious stories. They recognise features of religious life and practice, and some religious symbols and words. **They identify aspects of their own experience and feelings, what they find interesting or puzzling and of value and concern to themselves, in the religious material studied.**

Level 2
Pupils retell religious stories, identify some religious beliefs, teachings and practices, and know some are characteristic of more than one religion. They suggest meanings in religious symbols, language and stories. **They respond sensitively to others' experiences and feelings, including those with a faith, and to their values and concerns in relation to matters of right and wrong. They realise that some questions which cause people to wonder are difficult to answer.**

Level 3
For the religions studied, pupils describe some religious beliefs and teachings and their importance, and how some features are used or exemplified in festivals and practices. They make links between these and the ways in which religions express themselves. **They compare aspects of their own experiences and ideas about questions which are difficult to answer with those of others, and identify what influences their lives. They make links between values and commitments, including religious ones, and their own attitudes or behaviour.**

Level 4
Pupils describe the key beliefs and teachings of the religions studied, connecting them accurately with other features within them, and making some comparisons between religions. They show understanding of what belonging to religions involves, and how religious beliefs, ideas and feelings can be expressed in a variety of forms, giving meanings for some symbols, stories and language, using technical terminology. **They ask questions and suggest answers from their own and others' experiences about the significant experiences of key figures from the religions, puzzling aspects of life and moral and religious issues, making reference to the teaching of religions and showing understanding of why certain things are held to be right and wrong.**

Level 5
Pupils explain how some principal beliefs, teachings and selected features of religious life and practice are shared by different religions and how they make a difference to the lives of individuals and communities, showing how individuals and communities use different ways to express their religion. **They make informed responses to questions of identity and experience, meaning and purpose, and other people's values and commitments (including religious ones) in the light of their learning.**

Level 6
Pupils use their knowledge and understanding to explain the principal beliefs and teachings, what it means to belong to a faith community and how religious beliefs and ideas can be expressed in a variety of forms, in the context of different groupings, denominations and traditions for the religions studied, correctly employing technical terminology. **They explain clearly the experience of inspirational people and relate it to their own and others' lives. They explain clearly religious perspectives on questions of meaning and purpose and a range of contemporary moral issues, and relate these to their own and others' views.**

Level 7
Pupils relate religious beliefs, teachings, practices and lifestyles and their influence on individuals, communities and society to their historical and cultural contexts, to which they also relate the variety of forms of religious expression, including texts, figurative language, and symbolism. **They evaluate religious and other views on human identity and experience, questions of meaning and purpose and values and commitments using appropriate evidence and examples.**

Level 8
Pupils analyse and account for the influence of religious beliefs and teachings on individuals, communities and society, different views of religious practices and lifestyles and different interpretations of religious expression in texts, figurative language and symbolism, using appropriate evidence and examples. **They give an informed and well-argued account of their own views, values and commitments regarding identity and experience, questions of meaning and purpose and contemporary moral issues in the light of different religious and other views and feelings.**

Exceptional Performance
Pupils distinguish and actively explore different interpretations of the nature of religious belief and teaching, giving a balanced analysis of their sources, validity and significance; the importance for believers of religious practices and lifestyles and of the issues which are raised by their diversity within a plural society; and the meaning of language in religion in the light of philosophical questions about its status and function. **They place religious and non-religious views of human identity and experience, the nature of reality and religious and ethical theories concerning contemporary moral issues, within a comprehensive religious and philosophical context and make well-informed and reasoned judgements about their significance.**

A starting point: criterion-referenced assessment

The chart below picks out the 'skill words' from the eight-level scale. This is one way of looking at criterion-referenced assessment for RE, and perhaps a most helpful starting point. If pupils can increasingly use the skills specified here (in conjunction with increasing their access to concepts and content) then the standards of their RE work, and the progress they make, can be monitored and assessed in a straightforward way.

Level	Attainment Target 1: Learning about religions	Attainment Target 2: Learning from religion
1	Recount… Recognise…	Identify… (concerns, experiences)
2	Retell… Identify… Know that… Suggest meanings…	Respond sensitively… Realise difficulty…
3	Describe… Make links…	Compare (influences, ideas)… Make links…
4	Describe… Show understanding… Use technical terminology…	Ask questions… Suggest answers… Refer to religions…
5	Explain how… (share, make a difference, use differently)	Make informed responses in the light of their learning…
6	Explain… (with knowledge and understanding, in diverse contexts)	Respond by relating… (own and others' lives)
7	Relate… (historical and cultural contexts)	Evaluate… Use appropriate evidence and examples…
8	Analyse and account for… Use appropriate evidence and examples…	Give informed and well-argued accounts… …in the light of diverse religious views…
EP	Investigate and distinguish interpretations… Balanced analysis… (sources, philosophy, diversity).	Place religious ideas in comprehensive contexts… Make independent, informed and reasoned judgements…

Three examples of tasks and outcomes

The value of well thought out assessment tasks and criterion-referenced marking approaches is most clearly illustrated with examples of pupils' work. Here we present three examples, which show some good practice. Many more can be found on the QCA's website to exemplify the national curriculum (and RE) at www.ncaction.org.uk.

Example 1: Noah's prayers

Pupil A is aged 9.

Teaching and learning: This class worked on the Noah stories, meanings and symbolism through literacy activities. The themes of the story – danger, safety, promise, hope, environment, God's action and judgement – were the focus for discussion and writing activities.

Task: Pupils were asked to choose two key moments from a list of six in the story, and write prayers which Noah might have said at these key moments. Pupil A chose to write prayers about getting the animals into the ark and about the return of the dove with a leaf as the flood began to subside.

Level: In this piece of work, Pupil A gives evidence that she is beginning to be able to work at level 3. She can make links between religious story and aspects of her own understanding. She makes a link between religious values in the story and her own attitude of thankfulness.

Teacher's comment: Although Pupil A is only 9, this task has enabled her to show some good achievement. Both her letters are lively, but in the second one she uses two key religious ideas of the end of the Noah narrative: thanksgiving and salvation.

Comment

Literacy can enable pupils to show their achievement – this girl writes well. But assessment in RE must be to do with RE's objectives:

- Does she show understanding of the spiritual ideas in the story?
- Can she handle religious terminology?
- Can she identify the ideas of God in the story?

Noah's prayers: Getting the animals in.

Dear God,
    Please help me get the animals in. The elephants are so big, the snails are so slow and I'm missing a gazelle.
    Oh God help me! Please please What if there's not enough food? Oh no! Please Please PLEASE let it be Ok.

Amen

Noah's prayers: When he first saw the rainbow

Dear God,
    Thank you so much for keeping us safe thank you also for the beautiful rainbow! I will always remember how you saved us.

Amen

Example 2: Learning from the five pillars of Islam

Pupil B is aged 12.

Comment

This is an interesting example of learning from the five pillars because it required the pupils to make explicit links between their own experience and the experience of Muslims – this is difficult.

A clear structure enabled Pupil B to write thoughtfully about the comparison of two ways of life.

Teacher's comment: Islam is sometimes taught very factually. This activity aims to integrate the experience of the pupils with their learning about Islam, and is sound classroom work, rather than a 'bolt-on' extra.

Teaching and learning: Muhammad ﷺ asked Muslims to show their religion in five ways: something all the time, something daily, something when you're paid, something annually and something once in a lifetime. Drawing attention to this in a study of the five pillars, this teacher asked pupils to reflect on their own patterns of life in the light of their learning about Islam, aiming to provide opportunities to learn from the five pillars.

Task: This assessment activity asks pupils to relate the temporal aspect of each of the five pillars to their own intentions or ambitions. Beginning with discussion and a writing frame, this piece of personal writing was developed to make links between Muslim intentions and the pupil's own intentions.

Level: In this extract from a longer piece of work, Pupil B shows that she is able to work at level 5. She explains how beliefs and features of Islamic life make a difference to the lives of believers. She makes an informed response to the religious values and commitments of Muslims in the light of her own experience.

Learning about Islam

✶ All the time, Muslims believe that 'There is no God but Allah and Muhammad is His Messenger'. They say this many time during the day because it is the Declaration of Faith. It can also be known as the 'Shahadah'.

☾ Five times a day, Muslims intend to pray to Allah. They use a prayer mat and have many different prayer positions. They face Makkah as this is the birthplace of Muhammad and the Ka'bah (special holy building) is built there. They perform Wudu before praying. This is washing and they do it as a sign of washing away their sins. These 5 main prayers are called 'Salah'.

☾ When their wages come, good Muslims like to give 2.5% to charity or a needy cause. This may also be called 'Zakah'. They do this because they believe that all of their possessions, including money, belong to God and it should be shared among everyone. They believe that it is better for the money to be given secretly if possible so that people aren't seen to be wealthier than others. Farmers give 5% of their crops.

Learning from Islam

☾ All the time, I believe that you should treat others as you would like to be treated yourself. I learnt a saying in my old primary school, 'Good, better, best, Never let it rest, Until the good is better, And the better best'. This means you must always try your best at everything.

☾ Every day, I intend to get the most from every moment by trying my best in school and at home. I also try to do something worthwhile for another person like helping them, comforting them if they are sad or complimenting them on something that they have done.

☾ If I choose to be generous, I would give money to a charity such as 'Children In Need' because I think that everyone should get an equal chance in life. I would also hand down my old clothes, toys and other 'bits-and-bobs' to my cousin or a charity shop like 'Oxfam' or the 'British Heart Foundation' when they put the white bags for you to fill outside your front door. This would make me feel really good.

REtoday Services — *A Teacher's Handbook of Religious Education*

Example 3: Writing about beliefs
Pupil C is aged 12.

Teaching and learning: Pupils had studied beliefs about humanity, God and life after death in Hindu and Christian faith. Discussion had related these beliefs to their own ideas, and they were asked to concentrate on articulating and clarifying their own beliefs.

Task: This task was offered as a choice – the alternative was a factual explanation of beliefs studied. The choice is important and about 80% of pupils went for this more personal task. In 'examination conditions' but after preparation time allowed for homework, pupils wrote a piece of extended writing under the title 'My Beliefs'.

Level: Pupil C gives evidence that he is able to work at level 5. He makes an informed response to questions of identity and purpose in the light of his learning about religions.

Teacher comment: This assessment task needs setting and I found many pupils gave of their best through it. Extended writing doesn't help everyone, but many pupils need this chance to articulate their deeper ideas and responses. C is not at the top of the class academically, but this is a thoughtful piece of work, well expressed. I don't use many 'exam style tests' for this age-group, but this one works.

Comment

How much assessment is needed? RE should avoid over-assessing. In the 11–14 age-group, just one or two assessments per year which use the levels are enough to show progress in any pupil's learning. Better to have a few valid assessments than lots of invalid ones.

Generally in RE, **'Assess less, but do it better'** is a very good maxim.

My Beliefs

There is a subject that puzzles me, and that is God. I am not sure if I believe in God. After all, who is to say? We cannot see him, hear him or touch him. Having said that, I believe there is something out there that looks after us, looking over the world.

What I do not believe in is Adam and Eve. I think that this is just a story, made up with a moral to help people to be good. I think religion is something that everyone has to make up their own mind about. I have never felt that I needed God. When I was little, I thought I had to believe in God, but as I have got older, I have realised that it's a very personal thing. I thought I had to believe in God because we all said prayers in infant school. I got the idea it was something you had to do.

I don't really believe in Christening for this reason. I think people should be able to choose their own beliefs. It would be good to have a ceremony to welcome a baby into this world without being committed to a religion.

I think people pray, and it helps them, because they let their problems out, which makes it clearer and less complicated. Also they feel they are talking to someone, which makes them feel better. I think that's why people pray, and if it helps them, that's good.

I'm not sure if I believe in God, but if I don't, who says I have the right to celebrate Christmas? But I hope one day I can make a decision. I definitely believe there is something out there, watching over us.

Assessment activities

These examples of classroom assessment activities for RE are adaptable to different age-groups.

- **Can pupils** talk about religious topics? For example: What prayers would you answer if you were God? What makes a religious building special?

- **Can pupils** record their learning in pictures, charts, diagrams, photos or writing? For example: make a diagram showing what is important to Christians at Christmas; make maps and charts showing religious buildings in the local community, and key features of worship in each.

- **Can pupils** use the language of reflection to talk or write about how they feel, and how others might feel? For example: describe how the disciples felt when Jesus died, and when they found the empty tomb; express their own response to the beauty or awesomeness of nature; consider the feelings inspired by the *hajj* to Makkah.

- **Can pupils** pose and consider thoughtful questions about religious stories, rituals or beliefs? For example: Did Guru Nanak see God? Why do Hindus take presents to the gods and goddesses? What do Jews believe about the Hebrew Bible?

- **Can pupils** discuss a question, listening to each other and contributing in turn? For example: Why are there 300 churches in the city? What is the difference between a holiday and a Holy Day?

- **Can pupils** respond to religious dimensions of story with feeling and insight? For example: describe Moses at the burning bush; talk about the idea of self-sacrifice in *Dogger* (Shirley Hughes); write sensitively about the encounter with evil in *Tunes for Bears to Dance to* (Robert Cormier).

- **Can pupils** tackle a task which demands basic religious understanding? For example: choose Bible readings for a wedding, a baptism and a funeral; design a new mandir for their town, and plan an opening ceremony.

- **Can pupils** describe and interpret what happens in a religious ritual? For example: explain the meaning behind taking bread and wine at Eucharist, or facing Makkah to pray.

- **Can pupils** apply learning to new situations? For example, if Jesus cared for people and healed people of diseases, how might modern Christians respond to famine? As one of the commandments sets the Sabbath aside for rest, how should employers treat Jewish workers? In the light of Muhammad's care for animals, should Muslims join 'green' charities?

- **Can pupils** recall material they have studied and describe what they have learned? For example: describe the use of two different sacred texts; describe some meanings of a cross for Christians; explain some uses and features of *murtis* in Hinduism.

Recording achievement

In assessing RE, teachers aim to give **evidence** of all that each child has learned, understood and can do, in ways that are accurate, fair and informative.

Good practice is also **administratively lightweight**, not a paper-chase for the teacher.

RE policy works best where it **fits in with whole-school assessment**, recording and reporting policies.

At present, '**Assess less, but do it better**' is a good maxim for assessing RE.

So teachers might:

- give pupils tests to check their learning;

- grade pupils' work on tasks such as those given above;

- use individual record cards to record learning experiences and activities;

- get pupils to select their best RE work for keeping in a folder;

- take photographs or scans, or make audio or video tapes of pupils' performance (especially in group work);

- devise simple structures for self-assessment and peer assessment of skills, projects, creative activities, group work or other learning situations.

Introduction: Which religions?

Within Religious Education there is an inevitable tension between the two words 'religious' and 'education'. Historically it has always been the case that people were inducted into a particular faith community, not religiously educated in a range of faiths.

When the subject began to develop a truly educational rationale, it did so by distancing itself from its subject matter – religion. This led to an approach which emphasised learning about religions but was wary of any suggestion that pupils might learn from the religions they studied.

If, however, our concern is to facilitate the personal search of our pupils, we must expect that they will learn from the world faiths as well as learning about them. What we are trying to achieve in pupils has been described as critical solidarity – an ability to stand alongside the members of a faith community while still retaining objectivity.

As religious educators we tread a tightrope between engagement and objectivity. We have to see faiths as an insider would see them and retain the ability as educators to make judgements as to what, from which faiths, will offer our pupils the greatest possibilities for personal growth.

Selection and treatment

The RE Today Professional Services team takes the view that the **key issues** relate to the selection and treatment of materials from the faith communities.

The process of selection will, of course, already have started in the syllabus (for example, the LEA Agreed Syllabus), which may require certain elements of certain faiths to be addressed at particular stages. Many syllabuses, however, offer choices to schools which may leave them large measures of freedom.

Even where the content has been fairly tightly prescribed by the syllabus, there may be many different ways of treating it.

In Islam, for example, a treatment of *hajj* which focuses on the spiritual growth such a journey can inspire will be much more effective than one which concentrates almost entirely on mechanical details.

In deciding on the selection of material and its treatment, there are **two criteria** to be considered:

- Will this present a true picture of what is important to the members of the faith community itself?
- How much potential does this have for promoting the spiritual growth of pupils regardless of their own faith (or non-faith) stance?

A working code

The school might think about adopting a **policy statement** such as the one below with regard to the treatment of faith communities in RE.

With regard to the way in which it represents faith communities, the school will:

- **present** accurate information about the faith, both in its historical development and as it is practised today;

- **convey** how the faith is understood from within;

- **focus** on key beliefs, values and practices as identified by the faith community itself;

- **indicate** the variety of ways in which individual believers may respond to the demands of their faith;

- **involve**, as far as is practicable, practitioners of the faith to provide an authentic 'insider' view, while recognising that there may be a variety of 'insider' views;

- **endeavour** to achieve clarity about how faiths differ from one another while also pointing to areas of common ground.

Events in the past year have shown the great importance of educating our young people about the beliefs and the values of others. The need for a greater inter faith understanding has never been greater. RE has a pivotal role in helping young people develop respect for all and respect for truth.

Ken Boston, Chief Executive, QCA, 2002

Implications for methodology

An earlier section of this book has dealt with teaching methods and task-setting in RE but it is worth noting that the approach to world faiths identified here has unavoidable implications for methodology.

If the purpose of RE is to help pupils advance in their personal search for meaning through reflection on shared human experience and the insights of the major faiths, they are unlikely to achieve this through a heavily content-laden curriculum.

Pupils are most likely to advance in self-understanding by meeting with members of faith communities, by questioning, by reflecting, by imagining, by doing, by expressing.

The methodologies most appropriate for RE will be ones which engage the pupil in a process of discovery. Of course facts have their part to play in any programme of Religious Education, as in any other subject, but always the question needs to be asked: 'What will the pupil do with this fact?'

Questions for the RE classroom

What can be learned about:

- **writings** which are considered holy?
- **stories** told about God or the gods?
- **buildings** used for worship?
- **artefacts** and the meanings they convey?
- **ceremonies** and **celebrations**?
- **community life**?
- **faith being put into practice** in daily life?

What can be learned by asking:

- **what** does this mean to a believer?
- **how** might this change a believer's life?
- **what** beliefs, concepts or values does this practice point to?
- **how** does this relate to my search for significance?

Which pupil would you like to have taught?

Three pupils, having left different schools aged 16, fall into conversation at the job centre about their qualifications and schools...

Abby says,
'We did RE at school. I know loads about all the different religions. I think we studied about six, and although it was interesting to know what happens at a Buddhist funeral, I don't think it's going to help me get a job.'

Ben comments,
'It wasn't like that at our school: we did citizenship and careers along with a course about beliefs. I never really learned about particular religions very much, more just about issues like abortion and poverty. It was interesting, but I never knew why it was called religious education, really.'

Cassie says,
'I'm surprised - we didn't do many religions, just about Christians and Muslims, but it made me think a lot about my own ideals. I'm not religious myself, but I always enjoyed looking at the points of view in Christianity or Islam and reacting to them. I liked RE - it made me think about my own life more than any other subject.'

Christians

✝ Christianity – a brief outline

Christianity began in the first century CE as a radical element within Judaism. It is rooted in the life and teaching of Jesus of Nazareth, a first century Galilean Jew.

The early Jesus movements were linked strongly to Jewish life, but as the tradition spread it came to include Gentiles (those of non-Jewish background). With the conversion of the Roman Emperor Constantine in the early fourth century CE, Christianity became the official religion of the Roman Empire and spread rapidly throughout the world.

The essence (or core) of Christian belief is expressed in several creeds. **There are three main creeds:**

- The Apostles' Creed*;
- The Nicene Creed*;
- The Athanasian Creed.

The most commonly used and important.

The Apostles' Creed

I believe in God, the Father almighty,
creator of heaven and earth.

I believe in Jesus Christ, God's only Son, our Lord,
who was conceived by the Holy Spirit,
born of the Virgin Mary,
suffered under Pontius Pilate,
was crucified, died, and was buried;
he descended to the dead.
On the third day he rose again;
he ascended into heaven,
he is seated at the right hand of the Father,
and he will come to judge the living and the dead.

I believe in the Holy Spirit,
the holy catholic Church,
the communion of saints,
the forgiveness of sins,
the resurrection of the body,
and the life everlasting.   Amen

Jesus

The person of Jesus is **central** to all Christian belief and worship. Jesus is both a **historical** figure, and a person of **religious** significance.

Key features in Jesus' life:

- birth and childhood;
- baptism and temptations;
- call of disciples and continuing relationship with them;
- teaching through parables, miracles, the beatitudes and the great commandment;
- Holy Week (Palm Sunday to burial);
- resurrection, ascension and second coming.

Jesus and his teachings are expressed through:

- lives of Christians through the ages and today;
- worship, festivals, rituals and celebrations;
- how Jesus is portrayed in the arts;
- how belief in Jesus has influenced cultures and ways of life.

Denominations within Christianity

Over the course of history Christianity has broken up into a number of different churches or denominations. There are three broad groups:

The Orthodox Church

Mainly found in Eastern Europe, Russia and the Eastern Mediterranean.

The Roman Catholic Church

Found in all parts of the world, and accounting for some 60% of all Christians.

The Protestant Churches

Established as a result of the Reformation, and including the Church of England, Baptists, Methodists, Salvation Army, Quakers, and Presbyterians.

The Christian year

The Christian year begins with the first Sunday of Advent (the fourth Sunday before 25 December). The church has set out a cycle by which all the main events in the life of Jesus and the saints are thought about.

The most important festivals for Christians are: Easter, Pentecost and Christmas.

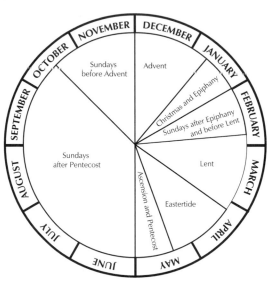

While the details of how Christians around the world celebrate these festivals may vary considerably, there are likely to be some common features:

- reading of and reflection on the festival story;
- special services and acts of devotion;
- symbols and artefacts;
- social events within the church community.

Christians today

Christianity was introduced into Britain from continental Europe in the early years of the Common Era, and is the largest and longest established of the world religions in the country.

The Christian tradition in the UK is ethnically and denominationally diverse, developing as immigrants brought with them their own distinctive traditions and expressions of faith.

Worldwide, Christians number around 1,999,564,000.

In Britain today, taking a broad view of membership, there are around 38,100,000 Christians.

The Bible

The Bible is a collection of 66 books. The canon (list) of books chosen for inclusion was decided in 397 CE. There are two sections:

The Old Testament (39 books)

Written over a period of some 1,000 years, this section includes: laws, myths, poetry, songs, prophecies, history and stories.

The New Testament (27 books)

Covering the period from the appearance of Jesus to the deaths of Peter and Paul in 64 CE, there are four types of literature: letters (epistles), gospels, history and prophecy.

All Christians refer to the Bible and regard it as a source of authority, but within different traditions or denominations there are a variety of ways in which it is read, understood, and followed.

The Apocrypha (15 writings)

Composed between 300 BCE and 100 CE, this disputed collection contains lengthy books, short letters and extracts. The writings may be included with the Old Testament, or printed as a separate section between the Old and New Testaments.

Christianity in the classroom

Christianity has a significant place in all syllabuses.

Teachers will be able to find many good classroom resources (such as books, posters, artefacts, CD-ROM, video and websites) to support engaging, challenging and active teaching.

A balanced programme of study should include material which aims to develop understanding of:

- Jesus as a historical person and focus of faith;
- Christianity as a world religion;
- teaching, beliefs and practices;
- festivals, rituals and practices.

The ideas on the next page suggest some activities for teachers with different age-groups to plan active RE work with a focus on Christianity.

Teaching methods need to be varied and stimulating, and draw liberally on the creative and expressive arts.

Work with 6–8-year-olds

- **Talk** about Jesus teaching his followers by using parables. **Ask**: What is Jesus' story?

- **Read** some of Jesus' parables. Use dance and drama to explore the meanings of Jesus' parables.

- **Visit** a church; talk with the vicar, minister or priest. **Use** these resources to explore the symbolism of artefacts. **Create** class guides to the local church.

- **Learn** about the Bible. **Ask**: How did the Bible come into being? How is the Bible understood and used by Christians in different times and places?

- **Join in** a simulation of a Christian festival or ceremony. **Ask**: What happens, when and why? Talk about feelings when joining in such celebrations.

- **Talk** about the importance of baptism for Christians. **Ask**: What is involved in belonging to a religion?

Work with 10–12-year-olds

- **Recognise** key symbols in Christian art, worship and language. **Ask**: How have Christians expressed their beliefs through the creative and expressive arts?

- **Compare** Christian places of worship. **Ask**: What is their significance in the lives of believers? What places are special to me? How do I show that they are special?

- **Read** about Jesus performing miracles. **Ask**: What makes something miraculous? **Create** a TV programme, including interviews with eyewitnesses.

- **Explore** the multicultural nature of Christianity, and its various denominations and traditions. **Ask**: How is this diversity reflected in the community where I live? In what ways will this affect me as I grow up?

Work with 14–16-year-olds

- **Debate** the extent of the impact of Jesus Christ on history, and on the current structure of Western society. To what extent has this impact been positive?

- **Explore** the concept of 'church' as outlined by Saint Paul. **Discuss** how 'church' today is understood and experienced within different denominations or traditions.

- **Interview** some practising Christians. **Identify** and **write about** the ways in which faith affects the way Christians live their lives today.

- **Discuss** and **evaluate** the extent to which contemporary culture in the UK is affecting the practice of Christianity. What are the implications for values in the lives of individual Christians?

- **Research** liberation theology and **evaluate** how far this approach to Christianity fits the character and teaching of Jesus. Was Jesus a liberation theologian?

- **Identify** the Bible passages which refer to the Christian belief in life after death. **Reflect** on your own beliefs. **Design** a piece of artwork to depict your feelings about life after death.

Muslims

Islam – a brief outline

The religion of Islam was revealed to the Prophet Muhammad ﷺ in the seventh century CE. The word Islam means **submission** or surrender, and the life of a Muslim is spent therefore submitting to Allah (God).

Muhammad (570–632 CE) was born in the Arabian city of Makkah where, from the age of 40, he received a series of revelations from **Allah**. The revelations were received over a period of 23 years, and were delivered by the Angel Jibril (Gabriel). These revelations form the **Qur'an**, the sacred text of Islam.

Muslims do not believe that Muhammad ﷺ brought a new faith. Rather, he is seen as the last of a long line of prophets sent by God to guide people on to the right path. Jesus (Isa) was one such prophet. Muhammad ﷺ is regarded by Muslims as the 'seal of the prophets'.

Those who accepted Muhammad ﷺ as the 'seal of the prophets' and his revelations as being from Allah, were welcomed into the Muslim community (**ummah**). This community migrated from Makkah to Madinah in 622 CE (the **hijrah**), a formative event in the history of Islam.

The Muslim way

Muslims regard Islam as a complete way of life (**din**).

There are **four main concepts** within Islam, which underpin all Muslim belief and behaviour:

- *tawhid*;
- *iman*;
- *ibadah*;
- *akhlaq*.

The **five pillars** provide a structure for the daily spiritual life of the Muslim.

Tawhid

Tawhid is the oneness of Allah. Islam teaches an absolute monotheism. To regard anyone or anything as being equal to Allah, or even a partner with Allah, is described as **shirk** and is absolutely forbidden. The Muslim profession of faith, the **Shahadah**, declares: 'There is no god except Allah.' This is not just an abstract theological statement but one which is worked out in many ways. God cannot be represented but the geometrical designs so prominent in Islamic culture are a reflection of the unity and beauty of Allah. And if God is one, the human race is one.

Iman

Iman is faith, the believer's response to God. Faith is expressed primarily in acceptance of Muhammad as the final messenger of God and of the **Qur'an** as the revealed word of God. Qur'an means 'reciting' and is the definitive guide for all Muslims. The *Shahadah* continues: 'There is no god except Allah; Muhammad is the messenger of Allah.'

Ibadah

Muslims use this single word for both **worship** and any **action** which is performed with the intention of obeying Allah. Thus worship and belief-in-action are inextricably linked by the very language. This concept covers many of the most obvious features of Islam, including prayer, fasting, pilgrimage and charitable giving. As the whole of life is worship, no special emphasis is placed on any one aspect of obligation. The five pillars provide a structure for the daily spiritual life of the Muslim.

Akhlaq

Akhlaq is a term which cannot be translated by a single English equivalent. It means both **behaviour** and the **attitudes and ethical codes** which lie behind specific forms of behaviour. Under this heading are included aspects of family and social life and also issues for the whole of humanity – for example, the possibility of an Islamic social and economic order which is a viable alternative to both capitalism and communism.

The five pillars

- *Shahadah*
  The declaration of faith

- *Salat*
  Ritual prayer carried out five times a day

- *Zakat*
  A welfare due, usually 2.5% of income

- *Sawm*
  A month of fasting (Ramadan) and spiritual discipline

- *Hajj*
  Pilgrimage to Makkah

Schools within Islam

There are two main schools within Islam:

Sunni Muslims

Sunnis (from **sunnat**, meaning tradition) believe that only they hold to the true faith as revealed to Muhammad. They maintain that leadership can only pass to a member of Muhammad's tribe (the Quraysh). Up to 90% of Muslims are Sunnis.

Shi'ah Muslims

Shi'ah Muslims maintain that leadership should only pass to the descendants of Ali (the cousin and son-in-law of Muhammad). Shi'ah means 'the party of Ali'. Shi'ah Muslims live mainly in Iraq, Lebanon, Iran and India.

Muslims today

From its origins in Arabia, Islam has spread to the Indian subcontinent, Africa, Malaysia, Indonesia, the Philippines and Europe.

Muslims have lived in the UK since the early nineteenth century. The largest Muslim communities are found in the West Midlands, Lancashire, West Yorkshire, Greater London and central Scotland. Most major towns and cities have a sizeable Muslim population.

Wordwide, Muslims number around 1,118,243,000.

In Britain today, there are between 1,000,000 and 1,500,000 Muslims.

The Qur'an and Hadith

Qur'an

The Qur'an (that which is read or **recited**) is regarded as the actual 'word of God', as revealed to Muhammad ﷺ. It gives guidance on all aspects of a Muslim's faith and behaviour, and covers a wide range of everyday topics.

Hadith

The *Hadith* (meaning **narrative** or **report**) is second in importance to the Qur'an. It contains records of the actions (**Sunnah**) and words of the Prophet Muhammad ﷺ and his closest friends. There are two broad types:

- **Prophetic *Hadith*** (the words and sayings of Muhammad himself);

- **Sacred *Hadith*** (their authority goes back through the Prophet to Allah himself; they were revealed but not included in the Qur'an).

Islam in the classroom

It is appropriate for pupils of any school age to study Islam. Many syllabuses require this, and others make it optional.

Teachers will be able to find a wide range of quality resources (such as books, posters, artefacts, CD-ROM, video and websites) for the engaging, challenging and active teaching of Islam.

A balanced programme of study should include material which aims to develop understanding of:

- Muhammad ﷺ;

- teaching, beliefs and values;

- sources of authority: Qur'an and Hadith;

- festivals, rituals and practices;

- Muslims in Britain today.

The ideas on the next page suggest some activities for teachers with different age-groups to plan active RE work with a focus on Islam. They are intended to be used flexibly.

Work with 6–8-year-olds

- **Listen** to stories about the life of Muhammad ﷺ. **Ask**: What do you think is special about Muhammad for Muslims?

- **Join in a simulation** of a Muslim festival or ceremony. What happens when and why? **Talk** about feelings when joining in such celebrations.

- **Talk** about how Muslims celebrate family life and the birth of a baby. **Ask**: What is special about belonging?

- **Watch** a video about *hajj*. **Think** about the ways in which *hajj* reminds Muslims that all people are of equal value. **Ask**: How might the world today be different if everybody believed this? Why do people find it hard to treat people equally?

- **Explore** the concept of special journeys. **Ask**: What is their significance for believers?

Work with 10–12-year-olds

- **Relate** the story of the revelation of the Qur'an to Muhammad ﷺ. **Ask**: Whom do pupils turn to for guidance? What books are special to them? How is the Qur'an used in the life of a Muslim?

- **Talk** about the *Shahadah* ('There is no god except Allah') and use the ninety-nine names of Allah to **explore** his attributes.

- **Focus** on the Muslim daily prayers (*salah*) as a time which Muslims set aside for the worship of Allah. **Ask**: What do pupils consider sufficiently important to set aside time for?

- **Explore** Islamic art looking at shape, pattern and colour. **Ask**: What is their significance for Muslims, in the context of *tawhid*?

Work with 14–16-year-olds

- **Consider** the implications of one God, one creation, one human race (*tawhid*). Can a Muslim be a racist or belong to an organisation like the National Front?

- **Reflect**: *Iman* is a Muslim's response in faith to Allah's revelation to Muhammad. What faith do pupils have? Who do they believe?

- **Discuss**: *Ibadah* is a response to Allah in worship and in daily living. How does this affect Muslim values and choices?

- **Consider** the concept of a society based on a religious code. **Debate**: What are the implications for individuals within an Islamic social and economic order?

- **Research** the role of women and men within Islam, and the importance of family life. **Evaluate** the extent to which Muhammad ﷺ can be considered a champion of equal rights.

Hindus

Hinduism – a brief outline

Hinduism dates back to around 1800 BCE, and has no single founder. The word 'Hindu' is related to a Sanskrit word, *Sindhu*, which is the name for the river known as Indus in English.

Hinduism is often called **Dharma** or the **Sanatan Dharma** (eternal way) by those who practise it.

The Hindu tradition is ancient in origin, diverse, inclusive and ever-changing. It may help in understanding the Hindu way to think of it as a huge river, with many streams flowing into it, flowing into a delta of many waterways flowing into the sea.

As in other religions, diversity plays a major part within Hinduism. Therefore, beliefs and practices vary according to:

* historical streams;
* geographical location;
* cultural traditions.

Similarly, there is a wide range of schools of thought, philosophical positions, religious practices and foci for devotion which are accepted.

However, within this diversity there are a number of beliefs and practices which are more commonly accepted, for example the authority of the **Vedas** (sacred texts).

The Hindu Way

The Hindu way has four aims (*punusharthas*):

* *dharma* (religious, moral or social duty);

* *artha* (economic development, providing for family and society by honest means);

* *kama* (regulated enjoyment of the pleasures and beauty of life);

* *moksha* (liberation from the round of birth and rebirth).

A Hindu is true to his or her *dharma* if all appropriate religious and moral duties are carried out.

Hindu beliefs

Dharma

The key concept of *dharma*, which sums up ideas about a person's social and religious duty, cannot be easily translated by a single English word, but it introduces other key terms in the Hindu vision of what it means to be human.

Brahman

Everything comes from **Brahman**, and ultimately returns to Brahman. **The One** is unknowable, and unapproachable, but humans can come to God through the many forms of gods and goddesses.

Atman

The Hindu concept of the human self, or *atman*, is important. The *atman* is the self (soul), that which pervades all things and which does not die.

Karma

The *atman* returns to the earth in another body according to the law of *karma*, or cause and effect. *Karma* is the total effect of one's actions, good and bad. All actions have their consequences.

Samsara

This cycle of reincarnation (*samsara*) sends the *atman* to live a duty or *dharma* in many lives in the search for liberation (*moksha*).

Dharma varies according to birth, and the circumstances of life, but the Hindu way values harmlessness to all living creatures and devotion to the divine and other people.

These values are expressed through, for example:

* a vegetarian diet;

* a commitment to non-violence;

* a close family structure;

* a way of life that makes time for worship and meditation.

Community, traditions and worship

The family community is an important focus for faith among Hindus.

Respect for older members of the family, a sense of belonging to a wider family and **caste** or *jati*, and the tradition of marking stages of life by rituals, and progressing in devotion or faith towards renunciation of earthly life, all combine to enrich Hindu community life.

It is in the **family** that the long tradition of worship, community and values is shared with each generation – often chiefly by mothers and wives – made alive in practice, and drawn upon for strength, security, peace and purpose.

Festivals typically draw family and community together. For example:

- *Shivaratri* (February/March)
- *Holi* (February/March)
- *Rama Navami* (March/April)
- *Janmashtami* (August/September)
- *Navaratri* (September/October)
- *Diwali* or *Deepawali* (October/November)

Hinduism today

The origins of the Sanatan Dharma are in ancient India, yet its contemporary expressions are to be found all over the world, in Africa, the Caribbean and Europe as well as in Asia.

The largest Hindu communities in the UK are in Greater London, Birmingham, Coventry and Leicester, and there are some 130 Hindu places of worship.

It is thought that 55%–70% of Hindus in the UK are of Gujurati origin, and 15%–20% of Punjabi origin. Wherever they are living, it is usual for Hindus to maintain links with their ancestral region and to speak their ancestral language among themselves.

It is very difficult to be accurate about the numbers of people who are Hindu, but responsible estimates suggest:

Worldwide: some 811,336,000, the vast majority living in India.

In Britain today: at least 400,000.

Sacred texts

Hindu faith is rooted in scriptures. A number of sacred texts, some revealed and some remembered (called **sruti** and **smrti** respectively), each have an important place.

The widest authority is attributed to the **Vedas**. The range of scriptures includes:

- social and ethical laws;
- philosophical material;
- hymns;
- epic stories of the gods and goddesses;
- poetry.

The use, discussion and interpretation of these scriptures enliven the Hindu community. For example, the **Bhagavad Gita**, a part of the epic **Mahabharata**, is often found in Hindu homes, wrapped in silk, read, learned and recited, and used as a source of guidance in life.

Hinduism in the classroom

It is appropriate for pupils of any school age to study Hinduism. Many syllabuses require this, and others make it optional.

There is no shortage of good quality curriculum materials for all key stages (such as books, posters, artefacts, CD-ROM, video and websites); many of the best of these include Hindu authors.

A balanced programme of study should include opportunities for pupils to think about:

- festivals;
- worship;
- stories from sacred texts;
- pilgrimage;
- the importance of the concepts and values which inspire the Hindu community.

Teaching methods need to be varied and stimulating, with an emphasis on the creative and expressive arts.

Work with 6–8-year-olds

- **Listen** to stories about Hindu children in Britain today, and about Hindu gods, goddesses and heroes.

- **Plan** the sharing of a dramatic version of a Hindu story to **present** to older children.

- **Talk** about the oldest and wisest stories and sayings they know, and **ask** parents and other adults to tell them such stories and sayings.

- **Practise** greetings (hello, bonjour, *namaste*, peace be with you and so on) and associated hand gestures: **learn** that the Hindu greeting *'Namaste'* means 'the divine spark in me greets the spark of God in you.'

- **Use** artefacts to see how all five senses are in use when a Hindu worships.

Work with 10–12-year-olds

- **Use** the creative and expressive arts as 'windows' into Hindu ideas about life. Examples could include **exploring** stories through dance; the use and symbolism of colour.

- **Visit** a Hindu place of worship (or receive a Hindu **visitor** to school) and take part in a question and answer session on Hindu ways of life.

- **Use** Hindu artefacts, particularly *murtis* of the gods and goddesses, along with Hindu stories, to **explore** symbols of the powers and attributes of the divine.

- **Make** pictorial charts of the life cycle, and **think** about both the rituals and the beliefs associated with our passing lives.

- **Explore** Hindu ideas about the knowledge and mystery of the divine, using creative strategies.

Work with 14–16-year-olds

- **Consider** key Hindu ideas of Brahman, *Atman*, *Dharma*, *Karma*, Reincarnation and *Moksha*. **Devise** diagrams to show how these ideas fit together.

- **Examine** the contours of the Hindu community in Britain, with reference to the diversity and flexibility of the tradition.

- **Explore** Hindu commitments to non-violence, harmlessness and vegetarian food. **Contrast** this with some Western attitudes. Reflect the example and teaching of major religious teachers in your response.

- **Ask** questions about the nature of the 'self', about what it means to be human, and **explore** Hindu answers to these questions.

- **Consider** the role of festivals within Hindu tradition, and the myths used at these times. How effective can these occasions be as a focus and prompt for personal reflection?

- **Investigate** the presence of Hinduism in the media (TV, radio, film, magazines, newspapers and the internet). **Consider** the advantages and disadvantages of religious events, stories and sacred writings being presented in these ways.

Buddhists

Buddhism – a brief outline

Buddhism was founded by an Indian Prince, Siddattha Gotama, who lived in the sixth century BCE. He was brought up in luxury, but when he encountered suffering he left his palace and spent his life in the search for answers to the questions posed by human life.

After following severe and ascetic practices for some years, he came to realise that a Middle Way of compassion to oneself and others leads to enlightenment. The path he taught to his followers for the remaining 40 years of his life showed a way to liberation from suffering.

Following his enlightenment at the age of 35, Siddattha Gotama was given the title 'Buddha' (meaning 'enlightened one') by his disciples. Another name which is given to him is *Shakyamuni* (meaning 'wise man of the Shakya clan').

The Buddha is greatly honoured for his teaching, but is not worshipped as God. Buddhists do not pray to Buddha. It is possible to be an atheist and follow the Buddhist path.

The Buddhist way

The Buddhist way involves:

- the **Four Noble Truths** (understanding the causes and cure of suffering);

- the **Noble Eightfold Path** (following a way of life which points the way to the end of suffering);

- **ethics** (precepts to follow);

- **meditation**.

The Three Treasures (Refuges)

Buddhists take refuge in three treasures:

- the **Buddha**;

- the ***Dhamma*** (the teaching);

- the ***Sangha*** (the community).

The Four Noble Truths

- **Life involves suffering (*dukkha*) until enlightenment.** It is not difficult to see that there is suffering and unhappiness in life, both in the world at large and within our own selves.

- **The causes of suffering are desires.** We do not like suffering and unhappiness: it is what we want to move away from. To do this, we need to understand and remove its causes.

- **The end of suffering (*niroda*) is possible – by replacing craving and desire with inner satisfaction.** The point at which this is achieved is called *Nirvana*, a state of peace and happiness. This is a goal which all can move towards.

- **Following the Eightfold Path leads to *Nirvana*, and the cessation of suffering.** This is the path of growth and development that enables us to cultivate the positive in all aspects of our lives. The Buddha warned in the *Dhammapada*, a famous Buddhist teaching, that it is the obligation of the individual to make the effort to follow this path.

The Noble Eightfold Path

• Right understanding	**steps to wisdom**
• Right thought	
• Right speech	**ethical steps**
• Right action	
• Right livelihood	
• Right effort	**mental steps**
• Right mindfulness	
• Right concentration	

Whilst Buddhist monks are often highly visible, most Buddhists follow the path as lay people. The community shares the task of alleviating suffering, supports its monks and nuns, recognises and supports its leaders and celebrates such festivals as *Wesak*, remembering the birth, enlightenment and passing away of the Buddha.

Many Buddhists do not attend Temples, but worship in shrines in their homes or gardens. This factor means that it is difficult to estimate accurately the true number of Buddhists in the world today.

Enlightenment

The unifying belief of all Buddhists is the enlightenment experience of the Buddha. Enlightenment is not a place, but a state of being, based on wisdom and compassion. It is to do with learning Truth for yourself.

Unless someone gains enlightenment, Buddhists believe that she or he will continue to be re-born. Breaking out of this cycle is known as *Nirvana*.

Schools within Buddhism

There are two main schools within Buddhism:

- **Theravada Buddhism**, meaning teachings of the elders;

- **Mahayana Buddhism**, meaning great vehicle.

Often, Theravada Buddhists will live as monks and nuns, free from the distractions of family commitments. Mahayana Buddhists believe that there are many ways of reaching enlightenment.

Buddhism today

From its beginnings in India, many schools and traditions developed within Buddhism. The Buddhist path is very influential in India, China, Japan, Thailand, Tibet, Burma, Sri Lanka and many other countries. Towards the end of the nineteenth century, Buddhism began to be practised in Britain, and Buddhist traditions from all of the above countries have found expression here.

Worldwide, Buddhists number around 360,000,000.

In Britain today, there are perhaps 130,000 Buddhists.

The Five Precepts (*Pansil*)

These are not commandments, but guidance to be followed by all Buddhists. They are not simply negatives, but encourage a positive moving forwards.

Buddhists should refrain from:

- harming or killing living beings;

- stealing;

- intoxicants (like alcohol, drugs or tobacco);

- sexual misconduct;

- wrong speech.

Monks and nuns have a further five precepts. They should also refrain from:

- eating after midday;

- dancing, singing and watching unsuitable entertainments;

- using scents or perfumes;

- sleeping on luxurious beds;

- handling gold or silver.

Buddhism in the classroom

It is appropriate for pupils of any school age to study Buddhism. Many syllabuses require this, and others make it optional.

Teachers will be able to find many good classroom resources (such as books, posters, artefacts, CD-ROM, video and websites) for the engaging, challenging and active teaching of Buddhism.

A balanced programme of study should include material which aims to develop understanding of:

- the Buddha;

- teaching, beliefs and values;

- festivals, rituals and practices;

- Buddhists in Britain today.

The ideas on the next page suggest some activities for teachers with different age-groups to plan active RE work with a focus on Buddhism. They are intended to be used flexibly.

Work with 6–8-year-olds

- **Listen** to stories. **Ask**: What happened to the young Prince Siddattha to make him leave his palace?

- **Explore** two images of the Buddha. **Ask**: Why do they look the way they do? What are they used for? Who values them?

- **Think** about not causing harm. **Talk** about killing and hurting. **Ask**: Why does this happen? Could it be stopped?

- **Make** a 'wheel' or 'stepping stones' pictures to illustrate the Eightfold Path. **Give examples** of what some of the steps on the path might mean in the playground, or in the family.

- **Consider** the symbols most commonly used for Buddhism – the wheel and the lotus flower. **Ask**: What can we learn about the beliefs of Buddhists from these symbols?

Work with 10–12-year-olds

- **Retell stories** of the Buddha's enlightenment, of his compassion, and of his followers.

- **Examine** artefacts, pictures, video and, if possible, a vihara to find out about meditation. **Compare** meditation with pupils' own ways of being peaceful

- **Create** collages of happiness, relating to different people, ages, origins and so on; use the collages to **explore** the limits to happiness, its impermanence.

- **Talk** about the Five Precepts. **Ask**: Would they make a perfect world? Do the pupils agree with them? Practise them? What five precepts would they offer the world? Do they keep these themselves?

- **Think** about the opposites to the Eightfold Path and discuss the meaning of each of the Buddhist steps, giving examples of the behaviour that would go with them.

- **Consider** together some of the key questions that Buddhism addresses. **Ask**: Can there be an end to suffering? What is true happiness? Where can humans turn for refuge?

Work with 14–16-year-olds

- **Examine** different ways of portraying the Buddha, and the meanings attached to them by the Buddhist community.

- **Consider** Buddhist answers to the question of suffering in **discussion**, **debate** or **interviews**.

- **Apply** the Buddha's 'prescription' for the ending of suffering to examples of social or personal problems.

- **Read** and **discuss** some of the Buddhist scriptures.

- **Study** the spread of Buddhism worldwide and the growing community in Britain from the viewpoints of history, sociology and Religious Studies.

- **Read about** or **meet** Western Buddhists.

- **Explore** Buddhist ethics as practised in the UK: for example, in prison chaplaincy or work with drug addicts.

- **Discuss** what it means to be a Buddhist and an atheist.

Jews

Judaism – a brief outline

Judaism is the oldest of the monotheistic religions, dating back to the time of Abraham (approximately 1900 BCE). He was called into a covenant with God to start a people that God described as numbering as many as the dust of the earth and the stars in the sky.

Jews believe in one God, the creator, beyond space and time, yet a very personal God, interested in humanity, and intimately involved with the world, caring for and loving creation.

Three areas of fundamental importance in Judaism are:

- **God**;
- the **Torah**;
- the **people and the land**.

God

Jews believe in one creator God who cares for all people. Jews worship God, saying blessings and thanks, and believe that God has chosen them to be the people of Israel.

Central to Jewish belief is the **Shema**, which begins with the words: 'Hear, O Israel: The LORD our God is one LORD; and you shall love the LORD your God with all your heart, and with all your soul, and with all your might' (Deuteronomy 6:4–5).

The *Shema* is written on parchment inside a **mezuzah** and attached to the doorposts of Jewish homes, to be remembered each time it is passed. It is also placed inside **tefillin** and strapped by some Jews to their forehead and left arm for prayer.

Yom Kippur, the Day of Atonement, is a very holy day when Jews fast and spend time repenting of their sins, restoring their relationship with God and with each other, giving them an opportunity to get closer to God.

The Torah

The **Torah** (meaning teaching, instruction or law) is extremely important to Jews. The term is used in a narrow sense to mean the first five books of the Hebrew Bible (Genesis, Exodus, Leviticus, Numbers and Deuteronomy) and in a wider sense to include the whole of the Hebrew Bible and the Talmud (see below).

At its heart is the message revealed to Moses for the Jewish people on Mount Sinai in the desert. It includes 613 *Mitzvot* (or laws), of which 365 are negative commandments, outlining what Jews should not do, and 248 are positive, things which Jews should do.

The whole Torah includes:

- the **TeNaKh**, or 'Written Torah', or Hebrew Bible, consisting of: the **Pentateuch** (Torah), the **Prophets** (*Nevi'im*) and the **Writings** (*Ketuvim*);

- the **Talmud**, or Oral Law, which is made up of the **Mishnah** (the first writing down of the oral tradition, about 200 CE) and the **Gemara** (a commentary on the *Mishnah*).

Jews regularly study the Torah: to do so is to worship God.

The Torah is held in great esteem and kept in a special place in the synagogue called the **ark**. A weekly portion is read aloud in the **Shabbat** synagogue service and there is an annual cycle of readings including all five books of the Torah.

Simchat Torah ('rejoicing in the Torah') celebrates the completion of the annual reading of the Torah. It is a joyful festival, held on the 23rd of the Jewish month of Tishrei. Torah scrolls are taken from the ark and carried or danced around the synagogue seven times. The concluding section of Deuteronomy is read, and immediately following, the opening section of Genesis, or *B'reishit* as it is called in Hebrew, is read.

The people and the land

Judaism teaches that people are made in God's image, and the family and home are very important in Judaism. **Shabbat** is celebrated at home on a Friday evening after dusk by a family meal, followed by a time of rest set aside to worship God and spend time together as a family.

Kashrut is the body of Jewish law dealing with the foods which are 'fit' to be eaten. These food laws go back more than 3,000 years to the time when God gave the Torah to Moses, and play an important part in the daily lives of many Jews. They are kept because the Torah requires it.

Food which meets the demands of *kashrut* is called **kosher**. 'Keeping kosher' involves eating only certain animals which have been killed in a special way. Meat and milk products must not be mixed; separate sets of kitchen utensils are used for these two types of food. Food which is forbidden is *treyfah* (or *treif*).

The **land of Israel** is also very important in Judaism. Although Jews live all over the world, Israel has always been a very special place for Judaism. Jews believe that this is the land promised to Abraham and his descendants, and that God led them to settle here. Later, King David established the kingdom of Israel with Jerusalem as its capital.

A part of the western wall of the second temple in Jerusalem is visited by pilgrim Jews, and some boys have their Bar Mitzvah there.

Jews today

Jews have long been associated with the UK, with the first Jewish settlers coming after the Norman conquest.

The UK Jewish population consists of both **Sephardi** (originally from Spain, Portugal and the Middle East) and **Ashkenazi** Jews (of central and east European origin), with Ashkenazi Jews being the larger group.

The largest Jewish communities are found in the Greater London area, Manchester, Leeds and Glasgow. There are also Jewish communities in Birmingham, Bournemouth, Brighton, Gateshead, Liverpool and Southend.

Worldwide, Jews number around 14,434,000.

In Britain today, there are around 283,000 Jews.

Schools within Judaism

There are two main schools within Judaism: orthodox and progressive. Both believe in the importance of the Torah, but they place different emphases on it.

- **Orthodox Jews** believe that both the Torah and the oral law contained in the Talmud have been revealed by God and as such contain God's unchanging words.

  Hasidic Jews come within the tradition of Orthodoxy. They follow the teachings of Israel ben Eliezer, also known as Baal Shem Tov, who took a mystical approach to Judaism.

- **Progressive Jews** (which includes Jews of both the Liberal and Reform traditions) believe that the Torah was inspired by God, but written down by humans according to God's will. Therefore they believe that God's law can be reinterpreted, and the laws brought up to date for today.

Masorti (Conservative) Jews emerged as a group at the beginning of the twentieth century. They may be thought of as halfway between Orthodox and Progressive Judaism. Masorti Jews aim to comply with as much of the Torah as is practicable in modern society, but may compromise in certain respects (for example, by driving to synagogue on the Sabbath).

Judaism in the classroom

It is appropriate for pupils of any school age to study Judaism. Many syllabuses require this, and others make it optional. When a syllabus gives choices, Judaism is sometimes chosen because of its close links with Christianity.

However, to share resources with Christianity and to base work solely on 'Old Testament' stories does not do justice to Judaism. It must be studied as a living faith in its own right, not as the roots of Christianity.

The ideas on the next page suggest some activities for teachers with different age-groups to plan active RE work with a focus on Judaism. They are intended to be used flexibly, and to draw upon the wide range of resources available on Judaism.

Work with 6–8-year-olds

- **Lay** a Friday night Shabbat table. **Ask**: What is the significance of each of the artefacts used?

- **Make** a spice box with household spices, and illustrate on the lid the thing pupils found most interesting about Shabbat.

- **Read and enact** the story behind the festival of Purim or Hanukkah. **Ask**: What do the stories reveal about the nature of God?

- **Discuss** the words and meaning of the Ten Commandments for Jews. **Write** and **draw** how they think people should behave towards others (and God if they wish).

- **Learn** about the *Shema*, and **write** a letter to remind Jews they should love and worship God.

- **Invite** a Jewish visitor into school. **Prepare** and **ask** questions about what being Jewish means in everyday life.

Work with 10–12-year-olds

- **Research** Jewish food and Shabbat laws and **plan** kosher menus for weekday and Shabbat meals. **Ask**: What is the significance of keeping kosher for Jews?

- **Compare** public and family worship. **Ask**: Why do pupils think family worship is so important to Jews?

- **Design** a mystery activity based on the Exodus and the need for the Ten Commandments, focusing on the need of rules for all societies. **Ask**: What would be the implications if the Decalogue was obeyed by all?

- **Design** a holiday brochure for non-Jewish visitors to Israel in which the following **questions** are addressed: What is the importance for Jews of visiting Jewish holy sites in Israel and Jerusalem? How might such a visit be different for non-Jews?

- **Find out** all the objects which Jews might have in their homes which identify them as being Jewish. **Ask**: What is the symbolism and significance of each?

Work with 14–16-year-olds

- **Compare** the ideas about God presented by Exodus, and by the scholar Maimonides. **Consider** how such contrasting ideas about God might be helpful. **Reflect** on your own ideas and questions about God.

- **Compare** the practices of Orthodox and Progressive Judaism. **Discuss**: How important are change, continuity and growth within the history of Judaism?

- **Analyse** the events which resulted in the *Shoah* (Holocaust). **Examine** the factors which result in racism and prejudice. **Suggest** how society could best deal with these issues, and include Jewish responses.

- **Consider** the part the concept of nationhood has played in the life of Jews. **Debate**: How far is it possible to separate religion from nationality?

Sikhs

Sikhism – a brief outline

Guru Nanak, the first of the ten Sikh gurus, lived in the Punjab region of India over 500 years ago. When he was about 30 years old, he received the call to preach the Word of God, and travelled extensively to fulfil this mission. Sikhism is seen as an original, revealed religion.

The **Ten Gurus** each contributed something to the developing faith and way of life that is the Sikh *dharma*.

The Gurus

- Guru Nanak (1469–1539)
- Guru Angad (1504–1552)
- Guru Amar Das (1479–1574)
- Guru Ram Das (1534–1581)
- Guru Arjan (1563–1606)
- Guru Hargobind (1595–1644)
- Guru Har Rai (1631–1661)
- Guru Har Krishan (1656–1664)
- Guru Tegh Bahadur (1622–1675)
- Guru Gobind Singh (1666–1708)

Guru Gobind Singh, the tenth Guru, founded the Sikh *Khalsa* at Baisakhi just over 300 years ago (April 1699 CE). It was on this occasion that he encouraged his followers to wear what are now known as the **five Ks**.

He also declared that the line of human gurus was to come to an end with him, and that the Sikh Scriptures were to be their living Guru.

The Gurus' teaching, now focused through the **Guru Granth Sahib**, emphasises belief in one God and the worship of the same, universal love, peace and equality, and the importance of service (*sewa*). Like Muslims, Sikhs believe in one God and, like Hindus, they believe in the cycle of birth, death and rebirth.

Sikh practices

Sikh practice includes:

- **using stories** from the Gurus' lives as examples of how to put faith into practice;

- **paying attention to** the Gurus' teaching and reciting the Guru Granth Sahib;

- **celebrating** festivals:
  - *Gurpurbs*, which are held in honour of one of the ten Gurus, to celebrate their life or death (for example, the birthdays of Guru Nanak and Guru Gobind Singh, and the martyrdoms of Guru Arjan and Guru Tegh Bahadur). Other anniversaries are also *gurpurbs* (for example, the installation of the Adi Granth in 1604 CE).

  - *Melas*, which coincide with important Hindu festivals but on which something important happened during the lives of one of the Gurus (for example, Divali when Guru Hargobind was freed from captivity and insisted on taking with him all other captives).

- **rituals** for:
  - naming;
  - turban-tying;
  - amrit;
  - marriage;
  - death.

The Sikh community

Sikh community is reinforced by:

- the Sikh Symbol, the *Khanda*;

- the *Khalsa*, or brotherhood of Amrit Sikhs;

- the wearing of the **five Ks** by some Sikhs;

- **worship** in the **gurdwara** and **sharing** in the *langar*;

- visiting the **Golden Temple** at Amritsar.

The Guru Granth Sahib

The scriptures were first compiled by **Guru Arjan**, the fifth Guru. He ordered that all the texts be brought to him. He corrected some, rejected others which were not by the Gurus and which did not contain the Sikh message, and added some songs and hymns. This task took over a year, and was completed in 1604 CE.

Guru Arjan's collection is called the **Adi Granth**, meaning 'first collection'.

Guru Gobind Singh revised the Adi Granth, adding the teaching of the ten Gurus along with those of other holy men. In this book, the **Guru Granth Sahib**, he told his followers they would find all the guidance and inspiration they needed to live out their lives as Sikhs.

All Sikh ceremonies and services take place in the presence of the Guru Granth Sahib, which is treated with the greatest respect and honour.

The gurdwara

The gurdwara, the home of the Guru, is a place of worship, housing the Guru Granth Sahib. This may be in someone's home, providing that they can care correctly for it. However, usually a gurdwara is a separate building which is used not only for worship but as a focus for the life of the Sikh community.

In the gurdwara, the Sikh ideal of equality is practised: anyone can participate in worship; no one is excluded; leading worship is open to all who can read the scriptures; all eat together in the *langar* (a free community kitchen).

Sikhs today

The first British gurdwara was opened in Shepherd's Bush in 1911 and there are now over 200 gurdwaras around the UK.

There are substantial Sikh populations in Greater London (especially Southall), Birmingham, Coventry, Leicester, Wolverhampton, Bradford, Cardiff and Glasgow.

Worldwide there are over 23,000,000 Sikhs, living mostly in the Punjab, but also spread all over the world.

In Britain today, there are over 350,000 Sikhs, making it the largest Sikh community outside the Punjab.

Sikh beliefs, values and ethics

There is one God,

- the supreme truth, creator and eternal (see the *Mool Mantar*).

Humans can find value in:

- remembering and meditating on the name of God (*Sat Nam*);
- honest work (*Kirat Karna*);
- charitable giving (*Vand Chhakna*);
- service of others (*Sewa*).

Ethical decisions are informed by:

- the principle of **equality**;
- *sewa* (This 'selfless service' is the outworking of the worship of God who is everywhere and in everyone.)

The use of any sort of **intoxicating drug** (alcohol, tobacco and illicit drugs) is forbidden to Amrit Sikhs. **Family life** is very important – **adultery** is thoroughly condemned and **divorce** is frowned upon. **Respect for and valuing life** is important since life comes from God.

Sikhism in the classroom

The study of Sikhism is appropriate for pupils of any school age. Many syllabuses require this, and others make it optional.

There are many sources of good resource material, such as books, posters, artefacts, CD-ROM, video and websites, for the engaging and active teaching of Sikhism. A balanced programme of study should include material about:

- the Gurus;
- Sikh beliefs and values;
- the gurdwara and community life;
- festivals, rituals and practices;
- Sikhs in Britain today.

The suggestions on the next page are designed to help teachers with different age-groups to plan active RE work with a focus on Sikhism. They are intended to be used flexibly.

CHESTER COLLEGE WARRINGTON LIBRARY

Work with 6–8-year-olds

- **Listen** to stories about the Gurus' lives or about Sikh children in Britain today – **respond** with questions and ideas. **Make** a 'zigzag' book with appropriate text and illustrations.

- **Join in a simulation** of a Sikh festival or ceremony. What happens, when and why? **Talk** about feelings when joining in such celebrations.

- **Look** carefully at artefacts like the *Khanda*. *Learn about* their symbolism and significance.

- **Think** about the idea that all people are of equal value. **Ask**: Is this happening in the world today? How can we help make the world a more equal place?

- **Make** a picture of a Sikh flag. **Discuss** its symbolism.

- **Give examples** of angry and greedy behaviour, but also of gentleness and generosity. **Ask**: Which would the Gurus approve of and which not? Why?

Work with 10–12-year-olds

- **Retell** stories of the Gurus in various visual, dramatic or written forms – **focus on** what Sikhs learn from such stories. **Ask**: What can I learn from them?

- **Make** collages on the theme of difference and equality. **Think** about the impact of Sikh teaching about equality on the way people in this country (or town, school or class) treat others. **Ask**: What would Guru Nanak say if he took our assembly?

- **Talk** about different Sikh names for God; **explore** ideas about God in other faiths and the pupils' own ideas. **Conduct** a survey about belief in God.

- **Make** booklets to illustrate a guided tour round a gurdwara, or a visit to Amritsar and the *Harimandir* (Golden Temple).

- **Examine** artefacts such as the five Ks and those associated with Amrit, and **write** about the value of these to Sikhs. **Talk** about what it means to belong and the symbols of belonging which pupils in the class have or use.

Work with 14–16-year-olds

- **Consider** questions of Sikh identity in modern British culture, from religious and sociological perspectives.

- **Examine** the story of Guru Nanak's disappearance and revelation of the divine, and **consider** Sikh interpretations of it. **Discuss** the meaning of 'God' and consider philosophical issues arising from it.

- **Devise** plans for a new, purpose-built gurdwara in the locality.

- **Read about** and **meet** British Sikhs.

- **Devise** various ethical and moral dilemmas – **explore how** Sikhs might respond, putting the teaching of the Gurus into practice.

Non-religious ethical life stances

Non-religious traditions in RE

Religious Education is not just for the religious, but for all pupils. Most pupils in schools in Britain today do not identify very closely, if at all, with a religious community, and so it is appropriate that RE should include consideration of some of the alternatives to religion which exist in our society. The myth that only religious people take ethics seriously is all too common; there are various philosophies and approaches to life which have nothing to do with any particular religion, but call followers to lives of love and unselfishness.

These living belief systems can be grouped together as '**non-religious ethical life stances**'. Their forms are often eclectic, but include everything from rationalist atheism and agnosticism, through post-Marxist accounts of humanity, to deliberately 'dis-traditioned' postmodern spiritualities or life stances.

People who feel at home with such descriptions do not all identify formally with humanism, but the British Humanist Association is perhaps the most visible and organised non-religious ethical life stance to be seen in the nation's public life.

If the RE field of enquiry includes an exploration of the experience we share as humans, and an opportunity for a pupil to take a personal search further, it follows that teachers can plan to consider beliefs and values, celebrations and ideas from ethical traditions such as humanism.

An ancient tradition

Humanism has a long history, and many great intellectuals from past centuries have influenced the modern humanist tradition. These figures would include thinkers from classical civilisation such as Epicurus and Seneca, as well as enlightenment philosophers from Thomas Paine through John Stuart Mill to Bertrand Russell.

Contemporary humanists in the UK include such public figures as Claire Rayner, George Melly and Professor Bernard Crick.

A community dimension

Though relatively few humanists belong to a humanist organisation (the British Humanist Association has about 4,000 members), the ideas of humanism are very influential in the UK today, and many people recognise themselves when they hear humanism described.

Humanism briefly described

Humanists are people who:

- believe primarily in humanity;

- hold that human nature is a remarkable product of the universe, but not the product of any divine creation, and that the human race can expect no help from the gods;

- place their confidence in the power of human reason, goodwill and science to solve the problems that face us, and reject the power of prayer or worship;

- accept the limitations of a lifetime and notice that we live on in the memories of others and in our achievements, but reject all ideas of rebirth, resurrection or eternal life;

- when it comes to ethics, believe that their own reasoned sense of goodness and happiness should guide them to decide what is right for themselves and others;

- are often concerned for the greatest happiness for the greatest number;

- think it is best to make ethical decisions by looking at the individual case, not just by applying a hard and fast rule;

- have often been active in working for human rights, and get involved in a variety of social and ethical issues.

I prefer to say that the spiritual elements which are usually styled divine are part and parcel of human nature. Sir Julian Huxley FRS

Those who identify themselves as humanist may have special secular welcomes for a new baby, wedding ceremonies based on humanist ideals and non-religious funerals. They may celebrate festivals in a secular way, whether this means joining in New Year celebrations with relish, or marking United Nations Day.

Humanism and ethics

Ethically, humanism is often personal and individual, liberal, tolerant and rationally based. Humanists may be in favour of free choice in matters such as euthanasia or divorce, and may emphasise virtues such as truthfulness, generosity, democracy, tolerance, justice and co-operation. Humanists try to put the '**golden rule**' into action: treat other people as you would like them to treat you.

Examples

There are relatively few published resources which deal explicitly with Humanism, particularly for the primary phase. Here are two examples (shown on the right) which might be useful for both RE teachers and pupils.

Non-religious traditions in the classroom

As RE explores human experience, beliefs and values, the non-religious approaches to life will be relevant at many points. Teachers can confidently include this material in the RE curriculum wherever it makes a contribution to the aims of RE.

Some syllabuses enable the planned study of traditions such as humanism, though many do not.

A balanced study of humanism should include:

• exploration of humanist beliefs and values;

• learning about some key historical and contemporary humanist figures;

• finding out about humanist activities and ceremonies.

Teaching methods need to be varied, challenging and stimulating.

With an approach to life based on humanity and reason, humanists recognise that moral values are properly founded on human nature and experience alone. We value the truth, and consider facts as well as feelings in reaching a judgement. Humanists reject the idea of any supernatural agency intervening to help or hinder us. British Humanist Association

Ten Non-Commandments

1 Never accept authority.

2 Base your conduct on simple, humane principles.

3 Strive to eliminate poverty.

4 Strive to eliminate war.

5 Do not be a snob.

6 In sexual behaviour, use your brains as well as your genitals, and always in that order.

7 Take the care necessary to enjoy family life and marriage.

8 Keep the law.

9 Commit yourself to active citizenship.

10 Have confidence in the modern world and your powers to improve it.

In 1964 the humanist Ronald Fletcher published a pamphlet called the 'Ten Non Commandments: A Humanist Decalogue'. **The text illustrates** the spirit and feel of humanism rather well, though, like other such texts, it requires a lot of unpacking and interpretation. It carries none of the authority of sacred texts in religious traditions – but the humanists would be proud of that. It is suitable for the learning needs of pupils from about age 12.

Five humanist slogans

One local group of humanists in Bromley has produced a set of posters to promote humanist ideas. They have the following slogans on them:

Good without God

Morals without religion

Rites without religion

Ceremonies without superstition

Ethical atheism

Work with 6–8-year-olds

- **Look** at the humanist symbol of the Happy Human. **Talk** about what makes people happy and sad. **Focus** (perhaps through role-play) on the ways people can help and support those who have sadness in their lives. Collage, cut and stick, or artwork might be produced.

- **Listen** to, and **talk** about, stories which exemplify human goodness without reference to any God.

- **Plan** and **participate in** celebrations of the work of 'secular' organisations which challenge injustice, care for the environment or guard human rights

- 'Do to others as you would like them to do to you.' **Draw** cartoons to illustrate the 'golden rule' when it works, and when it doesn't.

- **Compare** a 'secular' celebration like new year or a birthday with a religious one. **Ask**: What is the same, and what is different?

Work with 10–12-year-olds

- **Learn to use** the terms 'agnostic', 'atheist', 'secular' and 'non-religious' in speaking about issues of meaning, purpose and ethics in any RE context.

- 'Do to others as you would like them to do to you.' **Compare** versions of this rule found in many different contexts. **Apply** it to some moral problems. **Illustrate** how 'morality without God' can use this idea.

- **Examine** the ways humanists celebrate key steps through life and **explore** similarities and differences compared with religious ceremonies.

- **Use** the five humanist slogans on page 48 to get pupils to **think** about meanings, symbol and visual expression: ask them to **design** posters which illustrate the slogans, using non-religious symbolism and natural images.

- **Discuss**, **argue** or **debate** the reasons which humanists hold to support their rejection of religious ideas like God, prayer, revelation or life after death.

Work with 14–16-year-olds

- **Research** the ways key figures in humanism have put their ideas into action. Examples could include Thomas Paine, Simone de Beauvoir or Bertrand Russell.

- **Study** the 'Humanist Decalogue' (Fletcher) given on page 48. **Compare** it to some other codes for living, and **ask**: what if everyone lived like this? What kinds of families, schools, communities would we get?

- **Analyse** humanist ethical ideas and reasoning about issues such as sexuality, euthanasia or world poverty, and **articulate their own positions** on these issues.

- **Apply** Ninian Smart's seven dimensions of religion to humanism and analyse the question 'Is humanism a religion?' **Ask**: Does humanism have social, ethical, doctrinal, material, ritual, mythological and experiential dimensions? What are they? Is it a religion?

- **Discuss, analyse and respond to** the place of humanism in relation to world religions in an essay. A possible title: 'Pressure group or religious alternative: "Humanism in Britain is not really an alternative to religion. It's more like an anti-religious pressure group." How far do you agree that humanism is more like a pressure group than a religion?'

Status of RE: a checklist of questions

Building the status of RE is a continuous issue for our subject. In a secularising society, where religion is often ridiculed, RE can be marginalised. But the subject deserves better.

This page aims to help you think about how to build the status of RE in your school through a checklist of questions. Until the whole lot can be ticked, there is still a job to do.

While the list is aspirational, each of these things can be changed and improved by careful good practice.

Two uses for this list:

* **Development planning:** Use the list to analyse and set targets for your school's RE work to develop.

* **'Levelling the playing field':** Send a copy to your head teacher, curriculum manager or governors, with your comments.

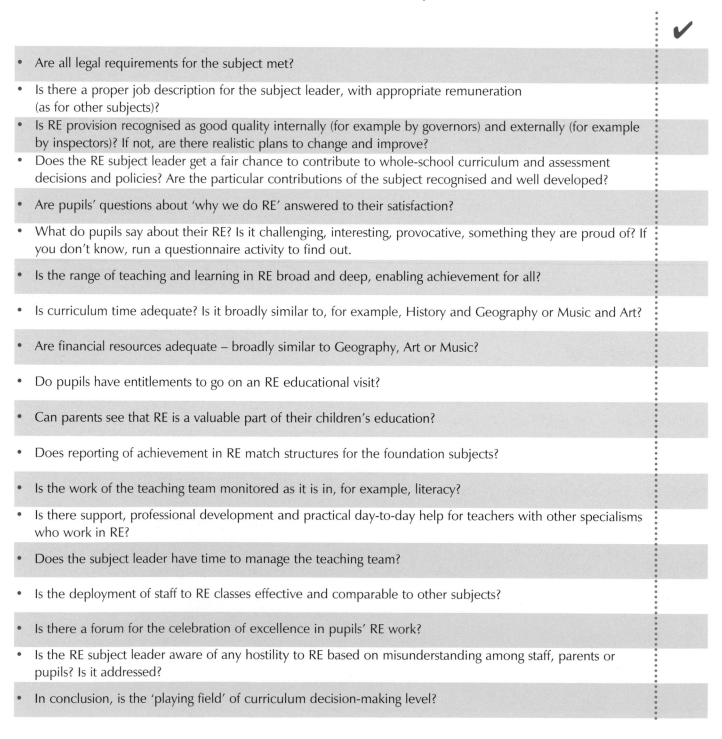

* Are all legal requirements for the subject met?

* Is there a proper job description for the subject leader, with appropriate remuneration (as for other subjects)?

* Is RE provision recognised as good quality internally (for example by governors) and externally (for example by inspectors)? If not, are there realistic plans to change and improve?

* Does the RE subject leader get a fair chance to contribute to whole-school curriculum and assessment decisions and policies? Are the particular contributions of the subject recognised and well developed?

* Are pupils' questions about 'why we do RE' answered to their satisfaction?

* What do pupils say about their RE? Is it challenging, interesting, provocative, something they are proud of? If you don't know, run a questionnaire activity to find out.

* Is the range of teaching and learning in RE broad and deep, enabling achievement for all?

* Is curriculum time adequate? Is it broadly similar to, for example, History and Geography or Music and Art?

* Are financial resources adequate – broadly similar to Geography, Art or Music?

* Do pupils have entitlements to go on an RE educational visit?

* Can parents see that RE is a valuable part of their children's education?

* Does reporting of achievement in RE match structures for the foundation subjects?

* Is the work of the teaching team monitored as it is in, for example, literacy?

* Is there support, professional development and practical day-to-day help for teachers with other specialisms who work in RE?

* Does the subject leader have time to manage the teaching team?

* Is the deployment of staff to RE classes effective and comparable to other subjects?

* Is there a forum for the celebration of excellence in pupils' RE work?

* Is the RE subject leader aware of any hostility to RE based on misunderstanding among staff, parents or pupils? Is it addressed?

* In conclusion, is the 'playing field' of curriculum decision-making level?

Foundation stage

Overview

Pupils are in the Foundation Stage from 3 years of age until they finish their Reception year, the year in which they have their 5th birthday.

Children aged 4 or 5 who are on the school roll in Reception class should be taught RE according to the appropriate syllabus, (for example the LEA Agreed Syllabus). This does not apply with regard to children who are withdrawn according to the wishes of their parents.

Although it is good practice to provide opportunities for children to explore RE material when they are in Nursery, there is no statutory requirement to teach RE prior to children entering the Reception class.

It is important that teachers note that the requirement for RE is different to the requirement for all the other subjects of the National Curriculum, in so far as RE becomes compulsory in the Reception class, when the rest of the curriculum is determined by the Early Learning Goals, whereas the rest of the National Curriculum starts in Year 1.

The information on this page (shown right) outlines the legal requirements in the early years.

The Foundation Stage

Guidelines provided for children who are in the Foundation Stage identify six areas of learning, known as the **Early Learning Goals**. These outline what children are expected to achieve by the end of their Reception year.

The six areas are:

- personal, social and emotional development;
- communication, language and literacy;
- mathematical development;
- knowledge and understanding of the world;
- physical development;
- creative development.

Foundation Stage: Nursery

- RE is non-statutory.
- Teachers may incorporate RE material into children's activities if they choose.
- Early Learning Goals outline what pupils should achieve by the end of Reception year.
- The National Curriculum is not expected to be taught.

Foundation Stage: Reception

- RE is a compulsory part of the basic curriculum for all Reception pupils.
- RE should be taught according to the locally agreed syllabus for RE or diocesan guidelines.
- Early Learning Goals outline what pupils should achieve by the end of Reception year.
- The National Curriculum is not expected to be taught.

Lower Primary: Year 1 and upwards

- RE is a compulsory part of the basic curriculum for all Lower Primary pupils.
- RE should be taught according to the locally agreed syllabus for RE or diocesan guidelines.
- The National Curriculum is taught alongside RE.

The Early Learning Goals are intended to provide the basis for planning, but are not a curriculum themselves. The RE programme of study must contribute to what the Early Learning Goals identify as expectations for learning.

The four areas of learning in the Early Learning Goals which most closely relate to RE are:

* personal, social and emotional development;
* communication, language and literacy;
* knowledge and understanding of the world;
* creative development.

The nursery

Activities which children participate in during their years in the nursery are experiences which provide the building blocks for their later development.

Starting with things that are familiar to children, and providing a variety of hands-on activities and learning plays an important role in children's learning at this stage.

Suggestions of RE activities in the nursery are shown on the right.

Themes which could provide opportunities for work in RE include:

* myself;
* my life;
* my senses;
* my special things;
* people special to me;
* people who help us;
* friendship;
* welcome;
* belonging;
* special places;
* special times;
* our community;
* special books;
* stories;
* the natural world.

The Reception class

In order to ensure schools are teaching RE in the Reception Class, teachers need to consult their syllabus for RE.

Activities for RE in the nursery

* creative play, make-believe, role-play, dance and drama;
* dressing up and acting out scenes from stories, celebrations or festivals;
* making and eating festival food;
* talking and listening to each other ;
* hearing and discussing stories – secular with a moral, religious or multicultural – which explore the inner world of thoughts and feelings, and which stimulate the imagination;
* exploring religious artefacts and 'soft toy' artefacts or books;
* seeing pictures, books and video of places of worship and meeting believers in class;
* playing with jigsaws depicting places of worship;
* listening to religious music;
* starting to introduce religious terminology;
* work on nature, growing and life cycles or harvest;
* seizing opportunities spontaneously or linking with topical, local events, for example:
  * celebrations;
  * festivals;
  * birth of a new baby;
  * weddings;
  * death of a pet.

Concepts

Concepts are the **key ideas** of any programme of study.

In RE there are two main types of concept:

- **General concepts** central to the shared human experience and the personal quest for meaning and purpose;

- **Religious concepts**, which fall into two categories:
  - concepts which are common to most or all major belief systems;
  - concepts which are distinctive of particular belief systems.

This diagram indicates some key concepts which arise in the RE fields of enquiry.

Whilst we have attempted to group related concepts together, this should not be regarded as definitive, as many concepts fall into more than one category.

Shared human experience ➡ Religious responses

Things we experience

Ways of expressing understanding and interpreting life experience

Life experience
community
commitment
celebration
freedom and authority
joy and suffering
change, loss, renewal
goodness and evil
motivation
relationship
spirituality
vision

Things which matter most to us

Values and commitment
love
compassion
respect
rights & responsibilities
service
stewardship
honesty & integrity
justice
peace
forgiveness
wholeness

Beliefs and teachings
God/deity
theism/atheism
revelation
interpretation
faith
commitment
holiness
morality
tradition
teachings of key figures
sacred texts
relationship with God

Things we strive to understand

Ultimate questions
authority
human nature
identity
meaning
origin, purpose, destiny
value

Religious practice and lifestyle

festival
worship
prayer
ritual
vocation
discipleship
meditation
devotion
reverence

Skills

Progress in Religious Education is dependent on the application and developing use of general educational skills and processes.

The following skills are central to RE and are reflected in a wide range of syllabuses, specifications and approaches to the subject. Teachers should plan to enable pupils to make progress in the use and application of these skills through each key stage.

RE skills	Examples of teaching and learning activities
Investigate – this includes the ability to: • **gather** information from a variety of sources; • **ask** relevant questions; • **know** what may be appropriate information.	• **Use a number** of textbooks or websites to select information. • **Highlight** the important information on a handout. • **Collect** leaflets from churches, charities and so on. • **Watch or listen** and make notes from video, audio or website. • **Write and ask** for information. • **Prepare** questions for a visitor.
Interpret – this includes the ability to: • **draw meaning** from, for example, artefacts, symbols, stories, works of art and poetry; • **interpret** religious language; • **suggest** meanings of religious texts.	• **Talk about** meaning in artefacts, pictures, paintings or symbols. • **Respond to** questions such as, 'What do you think it is?', 'What is going on?' (in a picture), or 'What issues does the story raise?' • **Use** figures of speech or metaphors to speak about religious ideas. • **Read** prayers and **talk about** what they show about the person's beliefs and feelings.
Reflect – this includes the ability to: • **ponder** feelings, relationships, experience, ultimate questions, beliefs and practices; • **think and speak** carefully about religious and spiritual topics.	• **Provide opportunities** for pupils to describe how atmosphere and actions make them feel. • **Take part in** stilling or guided visualisation activities. • **Use music** to explore feelings and thoughts. • **Write** a prayer a Jewish, Christian or Muslim child might use. • **Write** a poem. • **Keep** a reflective diary. • **Make** a 'wall of wisdom' to record pupils' insights.
Empathise – this includes the ability to: • **consider** the thoughts, feelings, experiences, beliefs and values of others; • **see** the world through someone else's eyes; • **develop** the power of the imagination to identify feelings such as love, forgiveness, sorrow, joy.	• **Respond to** a case study. • **Role-play** and freeze-frame – drama and mime activities. • **Fortune line or feelings graph** for one character (for example, Peter in Holy Week). • **Write** captions to pictures or slides. • **Tell** a story from another person's point of view. • **Answer** questions in the role of another person (hotseat).

RE skills	Examples of teaching and learning activities
Analyse – this includes the ability to: • **draw out** essential ideas, distinguish between opinion, belief and fact; • **distinguish** between key features of different faiths; • **recognise** similarities and differences.	• **Highlight** key words and beliefs on a handout. • **Identify** the 'odd one out'. • **Match** quotations to different faiths studied. • **Identify** differences and similarities between religious beliefs and practices within and between different faiths studied.
Synthesise – this includes the ability to: • **link** significant features of religion together in a coherent pattern; • **make** links between religion and human experience.	• **Notice** similarities between stories and practices from religions. • **Talk about** prayers, texts, places of worship and festivals, drawing conclusions about similar beliefs, values and practices.
Express – this includes the ability to: • **explain** concepts, rituals and practices; • **identify and express** matters of deep concern by a variety of means – not only through words; • **respond to** religious issues through a variety of media.	• **Creative**: drama, role-play, dance, mime, add percussion or actions to a religious story or song, make a game. • **Visual**: use of collage, colour, charts, diagrams, video. • **Oral**: use of audio tape, presentation or debate. • **Written**: poetry, reflective diary, letter, narrative story, newspaper report, questions for interview or visit, and so on.
Apply – this includes the ability to: • **apply** what has been learned from a religion to a new situation.	• **Write** a story to be acted out showing the meaning of a faith story or religious teaching in a different context. • **Design** own symbols. • **Respond to** a case study or dilemma – think about what Jesus, Guru Nanak, Buddha might do or say, what might a Muslim do … and so on.
Evaluate – this includes the ability to: • **draw conclusions** by reference to different views and using reason to support own ideas; • **debate** issues of religious significance with reference to experience, evidence and argument.	• **Use sorting and ranking** strategies such as diamond ranking statements according to what pupils think, or what a Muslim, Christian, Jew, Buddhist, Sikh or Hindu might think. • **Contribute** personal responses to statements relating to topics in RE ('can of worms' activity). • **Respond to** points of view on a scale of 1–10 (continuum activity).

Attitudes

Attitudes are not only explored in RE, they are also experienced. Teachers cannot operate without promoting some attitudes and discouraging others.

It is good practice to be clear about the attitudes needed for pupils to flourish in RE and to reflect on how the attitudes pupils experience in school are consistent with these.

RE should help pupils to develop positive attitudes towards self, others, society and the world, as shown in the diagram below.

For teachers to think about

Is my classroom a place where:

- each pupil's identity (personal, religious, cultural) is affirmed?
- each pupil is praised whenever they do something praiseworthy?
- each pupil is encouraged to express their own insights and is listened to?
- ridicule or scorn is totally unacceptable?
- adults set personal examples of integrity by being truthful in all respects, even admitting ignorance or uncertainty when necessary?

Attitudes towards living in a religiously plural and multicultural society

The development of...

an appreciation of religion as a fundamental element in human experience and a recognition of the value of different ways of looking at life;

recognition that truth can be expressed in many forms and not only in the literal, the historical or the scientific.

Attitudes to others

The development of...

respect for those who have different beliefs, practices and life-stances from oneself;

willingness to recognise the right of others to have different opinions and behave in different ways;

determination to avoid scorn in response to the deeply felt convictions of others;

willingness to learn from the insights of others;

willingness to defend for others all the rights which we claim for ourselves.

Attitudes towards oneself

The development of....

a mature sense of self-worth, enabling pupils to be confident in their own capacity to reflect and offer their own insights and questions of meaning and purpose;

a strong sense of identity: confidence and appreciation of personal, family, cultural and religious values;

willingness to listen and consider views of others whilst not being readily swayed by them;

willingness to acknowledge the possibility of being wrong, biased or prejudiced;

personal integrity in living by one's beliefs and values.

Attitudes to the world

The development of...

a sense of wonder at the vastness, beauty and mystery of the universe;

recognition of the interdependence of all life forms on earth and the need for individual responsibility;

recognition that material gain is not the only goal in life and willingness to look for spiritual values as the basis for action.

Thinking skills

New classroom strategies for religious learning are always exciting, because they provide ways of engaging pupils that are fresh.

In recent years, through academic development and government action, the group of strategies called 'thinking skills' are a source of energetic innovation in the RE curriculum.

If RE can enable pupils to '**think about thinking**' and to 'learn how to learn' then the subject can make a great contribution to general educational standards and also to the ways in which each pupil deepens their understanding of religious and spiritual questions. This makes it worthwhile for any teacher of RE to investigate some thinking skills strategies.

The role of the teacher in promoting thinking is central: below are expressed some of the kinds of questions teachers use a lot if they want to prioritise thinking as a skill set in the RE classroom. They are expressed generally, but have obvious and specific connections to huge amounts of the content of RE.

> *RE is an academic subject ... a rigorous activity involving a variety of intellectual disciplines ... thinking skills of research, selection, analysis, interpretation, reflection, empathy, synthesis, application, expression and communication are promoted.* (QCA Non Statutory RE Guidance, 2000)

> *Teachers can enable pupils to think better, more deeply, more productively and with insight, clarity, wide awareness and reasoned judgement. In RE these kinds of thinking are essential, and our interest in general 'thinking about thinking' strategies from every source is keen because we need to make our subject a 'thinking centre' within the whole curriculum.*
>
> (Professional Council for RE Action Group on thinking skills in RE, 2001)

Process questions
(to help pupils attend to how they learn)

- What have you been thinking about?
- What is puzzling about this?
- What makes people argue about this?
- Why do people hold this belief?
- How do you see it?
- Can you give an example to prove your point?
- Can you give an experience of your own as evidence of that?

Speculative questions

- What do you think would happen if...?
- In the future, how will this change?
- What do you think they were thinking, intending or hoping for?
- Can you guess what happens next?
- What do you think a prophet, guru, swami or deity would say about this?
- If you were faced with this belief, custom, tradition or challenge, how would you respond?

Connecting questions
(to help holistic understandings to emerge)

- What do you know that is similar to this?
- What makes this belief, practice or idea unique or distinctive?
- Does anything similar to this happen in your life, family, culture or society?
- Why is this idea, practice or belief important in this religion?
- What shared human experiences lie underneath this specific religious example?
- Does this piece of RE show that we are all the same, or all different?

Questions about thinking itself
(Meta-cognitive questions)

- How did you come to that view?
- Were there steps in your thinking here? What were they?
- Did visualising help you to think this out?
- How has your own thinking changed?
- Who helped you understand?
- Can you describe how you reached this conclusion?
- What advice would you give to someone starting this work next lesson? Why?

What makes for effective use of thinking skills in RE? Six key elements

Clear objectives	Be precise about the gains in learning and the skills being practised. What do you intend that pupils will be thinking about?	Not 'know six terms about Sikh worship' but 'be able to apply three general terms about worship to Sikh practice'.
Articulation	Get pupils to express their thoughts in their words – spoken and written. 'What do you think?' is the most important RE question.	Not 'take the information given and "return to sender"' but 'put together arguments, issues, experiences of your own'. Key role of language in learning.
Mediation	The teacher's role is between the learner and the content, extending understanding through questions, tasks, prompts or facilitating connections.	Not 'I'm telling you what I know' but 'you're in a thoughtful process: I can help you make it work better, try this'.
Connecting learning	Seeing increasingly what it means to widen and deepen the picture of religion and life which the learner works with.	The teacher doesn't do the connecting, but opens the channels, seeking to enable holistic connection all the time.
Evaluation	Being enabled to judge, weigh up, see strengths and weaknesses. Being happy to be tentative.	Not a formulaic listing of points for and against, but a deepening recognition that big questions are contested and answers vary, but one's own answer matters greatly.
Meta-cognition	Think about thinking: process questions and tasks which make it possible to 'do better', to philosophise, to be a more self-aware and critically engaged learner about and from religion.	So teachers don't rush on to the next bit of content, but pause to examine how we did that, and what did that contribute to our skills in theology, philosophy or RS.

Three simple examples of 'thinking skills' strategies for RE

What matters most to Christians?

A class of **7-year-old pupils** have studied Christianity for a term. The teacher provides twenty cards with objects, people or ideas from Christianity to trios of pupils, and sets the discussion task of ranking them: What matters most to Christians; what matters less? The follow-up task asks pupils to list seven things that matter most to them. **The aim** is to get younger children engaged in evaluating the significance of what they have learned about Christianity, and relating it to what is significant in their own lives.

What happened to Guru Nanak when he disappeared?

A class of **11-year-old pupils** are given twelve clues from which to create some answers to this question ('a mystery'). They work in pairs from the clues given – which include some red herrings – to hypothesise and speculate about the strange events of the start of Sikhism. After arguing their case, they compare their answers with what Sikhs say about the story. **The aim** is to engage with a key event in the origins of Sikhism through speculation.

Is God? Weighing up some arguments

A class of **14-year-old pupils** are put in groups of five to prepare their one spokesperson to support one argument for or against the reality of God. Equipped with a range of statements of the argument, they rank and order them to see which is most persuasive, and then conduct a 'mental fight' between the six groups to find a 'winning argument'. **The aim** is to get older pupils to articulate strengths and weaknesses of arguments they do and don't adopt for themselves, connecting their learning to a major religious question.

Creativity: RE and the creative arts

The development of the imagination is a key to all learning.

Imagination in science, in maths, in medicine, leads to new discoveries and to new methods of working. In education, the development of the imagination enables understanding, so that real learning can take place.

In RE, and particularly the area of the subject which is to do with 'learning from religion', the use of creative and expressive arts emphasises the development of emotional and spiritual intelligence. They involve all the senses in a first-hand way and open up learning rather than restrict opportunities.

Using creative and expressive arts in education is like using a kaleidoscope – it brings everything alive and provides endless possibilities.

A range of RE skills are enhanced by the development of the imagination and its expression:

- investigation;
- enquiry;
- exploration;
- evaluation;
- empathy;
- reflection and response.

Research has shown that developing active learning strategies which engage pupils in creative tasks is an effective motivator. Educating the whole child becomes a reality as they acquire and develop their use of vocabulary to describe their feelings. Belief in their own self-worth grows when they realise that emotional and spiritual responses are both expected and valued and develop the confidence to express themselves.

The creation of something new is not accomplished by the intellect alone but by the play instinct. The creative mind plays with the objects it loves. C G Jung

With regard to RE, we might note:

- Religions revere and stimulate creativity in their most radical and dynamic forms.

- Much can be learned about religion by exploring the creativity within it. Beliefs are often embedded within the creative expressions of believers, and it can be through creative expression that believers worship.

- Many religions exalt the divine creativity, and see human creativity as exalted.

- Aesthetic diversity is normal within religions, but word, image, symbol, vision often energise spiritual life within religions, and beyond them all.

- RE's long-term curriculum partnership is in humanities, and this will continue. But the new frontier with creative and expressive arts is where much new energy can be found, and is a key for the future.

- RE is endangered by dry factuality at the present: the springs of creativity are needed by the teachers of RE.

- Pupil tasks in RE are good if they extend, challenge, engage and inspire, bad if they close down, are too easy, seem irrelevant and bore. Creative demands tend to the former list.

- Learning from religion and creative engagement share a key feature: you can't do it without responding for yourself.

- RE, like religion, like life, is meaning-making activity. That's a creative process for humans.

Look and you will find it. What is unsought will go undetected. Sophocles

Imagination is more important than knowledge. Albert Einstein

The planning process

Planning for creativity within RE is vital. It is important to:

- **identify the learning objective or outcome.** Will this allow for emotional or spiritual development? What skills do you hope to address? Will the tasks help pupils to achieve the stated outcomes?

- **consider the lesson stimulus.** How will pupil interest be engaged? Is there an activity to which all pupils can respond?

- **ensure the task is open to different forms of expression.** Are words such as express, imagine and describe used?

- **decide the nature of the choice of activities offered.** Is a free choice of creative activities centred around the task appropriate? Or would directed choice better meet the learning objective?

- **identify those pupils who need tasks broken down into smaller units or incremental goals.** How would you identify the main characters in a piece of drama, for example? How will you introduce them? How will you develop the plot? How will it end?

- **identify those pupils who are struggling because they have not developed skills necessary to engage with the task.** How will you develop the necessary skills? Do you need to offer an alternative? Is the task inappropriate at this stage, or for this pupil, or for the group?

- **encourage pupils to try new skills by creating a classroom environment which praises endeavour as well as achievement.** Which frameworks would help pupils feel secure? How do you ensure that pupils know and understand what is expected of them?

- **recognise the achievement of pupils.** How can work be effectively displayed, and where? What guidelines for marking work are there, and are they appropriate for all types of work?

- **provide opportunities for pupil evaluation.** What did they think and how did they feel about the task, the lesson, their efforts and achievements?

- **plan for assessment.** How do you ensure that it is the RE element that is assessed, not the creative presentation?

> *Being creative is seeing the same thing as everybody else but thinking of something different.*

Creativity is defined as imaginative activity fashioned so as to produce outcomes that are both original and of value. Creativity is understood as something which is diverse and multifaceted, possible in all fields of human intelligence, not just the arts; existing in all people in one form or another. The creative processes are developed through practical application and in all subject areas. They require pupils to learn control, techniques, knowledge, skills, understanding as well as having the freedom and confidence to experiment.

(All Our Futures: Creative and cultural education – a report commissioned by the Government, chaired by Professor Ken Robinson, published in 1999)

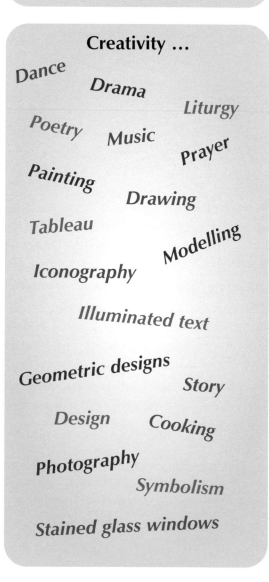

Creativity ...

Dance
Drama
Liturgy
Poetry   Music
Prayer
Painting
Drawing
Tableau
Modelling
Iconography
Illuminated text
Geometric designs
Story
Design   Cooking
Photography
Symbolism
Stained glass windows

Literacy and RE

Why consider literacy issues in RE (and vice versa)?

- RE is a language-saturated subject.

- Improved language and literacy skills enable pupils to gain:

  - more from their work in RE;

  - opportunities to apply, extend and reinforce learning from one part of the curriculum to another.

But...

- RE must not be driven by literacy objectives;

- RE must be planned and delivered in accordance with the syllabus relevant to the school;

- RE learning objectives must be central to work in RE.

RE offers a range of texts

RE provides opportunities for pupils to encounter a range of different types of text. For example:

- traditional stories from a range of cultural backgrounds;

- parables and myth;

- biography;

- stories that raise moral and ethical issues;

- discussion texts;

- poetry.

In addition, the use of non-fiction textbooks in RE enhances pupils' general literacy skills.

In literary terms, texts are divided broadly into 'fiction and poetry' and 'non-fiction'. Whilst RE text and information books and 'secular stories' with an RE theme 'fit' into these categories, it is not so clear where, for example, stories from the sacred texts of faith communities 'fit'. On one level they can be categorised as traditional or poetry or parable, but there is a deeper level of meaning for members of those faith communities. To categorise them purely in literary terms does them a disservice.

RE must allow for the religious significance and meaning of the text to be explored.

> *Story grows out of life, reflects it and enters into dialogue with it. All life is in story so that their children will find their experience confirmed, challenged, developed and broadened.* Maurice Lynch

RE and 'types' of story

There are two main types of story focused on in RE.

'Sacred stories'

Sacred stories, or stories from faith communities, may:

- come from the scriptures of a particular religion;

- be about a spiritual leader or founder of a faith;

- offer insight into the beliefs and practices of a faith.

'Secular stories'

These are stories with no explicit religious instigation or expression but which nevertheless address themes, ideas and concepts which religious traditions also address.

Secular stories can become 'ways into' understanding religious ideas and concepts.

> *Literature can help re-create inwardly that shared sense of being human without which our world would truly be a wilderness, a chaos.* Richard Hoggart

Developing reading and writing or speaking and listening in RE

The following questions act as 'prompts' for teachers to consider how they can improve specific literacy skills in and through RE and at the same time improve the quality of the expression of the pupils (written and oral) in RE.

Reading and writing

- In RE, what opportunities do we give to our pupils to allow them to read and write with confidence, fluency and understanding?

- How do we encourage them to have an interest in words and their meanings and a growing vocabulary?

- How do we introduce them to subject-specific words and help them understand them?

- What is the range of writing we offer them as part of their work in RE?

- Do we provide them with a range of different types of text?

- Do we ask them to compare and contrast different accounts of the same incident?

- Do they consider expression and bias?

- Do we ask them to respond in a range of different ways – for example, comprehension, précis, story writing, writing for different audiences, poetry, essay writing, project writing, report writing?

- How does what we offer compare with the range offered in and through other areas of the curriculum?

In RE, pupils encounter a range of distinctive forms of written and spoken language, including sacred texts, stories, history, poetry, creeds, liturgy and worship, linked to fundamental human needs and aspirations.
RE has distinctive concepts and terminology, which stimulate pupils to use their language skills...
In particular, pupils learn to talk and write with knowledge and understanding about religious and other beliefs and values, to discuss many of the fundamental questions of life ... and to present information and ideas.

QCA non-statutory guidance on RE, 2000

Speaking and listening

How often do pupils have the chance to speak about an issue in a pair, in a small group (three to five) or as a class?

- How confidently do they do that?

- How can we increase their confidence?

Can individual pupils present information and ideas about religious and moral issues to the class orally?

- How do we increase opportunities for them to do so?

- How do we increase their ability to do so?

Do our pupils listen carefully and respectfully to others?

- Do they understand what is being said and use it to further discussion?

- Can our pupils put 'both sides of an argument'?

- Can they give valid reasons for their opinions in an articulate way?

I love the open discussion we have in our RE lessons. Expressing your opinions is a valuable way of communication and improving your communication skills.

14-year-old, male

RE, Citizenship and PSHE

RE provides many opportunities for pupils to develop social and interpersonal skills and to increase their understanding of human relationships and responsibilities within society.

In these and other ways RE can make a significant contribution to Citizenship and PSHE.

Provision for RE should be clearly identifiable and distinct from other curriculum areas. It is important, however, to recognise that productive links may be made between RE, PSHE and Citizenship, both in content and approaches to learning, and that RE can make a substantial contribution to pupils' development both personally and as young citizens.

When planning the curriculum, schools need to ensure that RE is not driven by PSHE or Citizenship objectives. It must be planned in accordance with the RE syllabus, with RE learning objectives paramount.

The table below indicates some of the ways in which RE can contribute.

Some aspects of Citizenship and Personal, Social and Health Education	RE provides opportunities for pupils to:
Personal development – this concerns... helping pupils lead confident, healthy and responsible lives as individuals and members of society, gaining practical knowledge and skills to help them live healthily and deal with the spiritual, moral, social and cultural issues they face as they mature.	• **develop** understanding and awareness of beliefs and values and how these motivate and guide actions at personal and community level.
Global citizenship – this concerns... enabling pupils to understand their rights and responsibilities as members of a global community; issues of social justice and equality, diversity, interdependence, peace and conflict and sustainable development.	• **gain** knowledge and understanding of beliefs, practices and lifestyles at local, national and global levels; • **reflect** on the values and intentions that underpin human actions.
Education for racial equality and community cohesion – this concerns...... enabling pupils to develop attitudes of tolerance and respect for those who see the world in a different way to themselves, and promoting dialogue between pupils about issues of belief, community and religion.	• **develop** knowledge, understanding and respect for different religious beliefs, values, traditions and ethical life stances; • **explore** issues of equality, justice, prejudice and discrimination, and the religious teachings and responses to these issues.
Education for sustainable development and environmental awareness – this concerns..... enabling pupils to participate in decisions that will improve the quality of life without damaging the planet for future generations. **Key concepts** include stewardship, needs, rights, responsibilities, values and sustainability.	• **reflect** on how humans treat each other and their environment; • **explore** beliefs and teachings of world faiths on the origin and value of life.

RE and Spiritual, Moral, Social and Cultural Development (SMSC)

RE makes a significant contribution to pupils' personal development in all aspects, but particularly to spiritual development.

RE is concerned with the ways in which people express their understanding of the significance and purpose of life, and is uniquely placed to promote the personal development of pupils through:

- its distinctive content, exploring the teachings, beliefs and values of world faiths for insights into the nature and purpose of existence;

- the learning experiences, resources, styles of teaching and the personal interaction essential to learning about and learning from religion.

The table below indicates some of the ways in which RE can contribute.

Aspects of pupils' personal development	RE provides opportunities for pupils to:
Spiritual development – this concerns... pupils' developing competence in knowledge and insights into beliefs, values and principles and ability to reflect on aspects of their own lives.	• **consider** life's fundamental questions and how religious teaching can relate to them; • **explore and respond** to such questions with reference to the teaching and practices of religions, and from their own experience and viewpoint; • **reflect** on and express their own beliefs, values and principles in the light of what they are studying in RE.
Moral development – this concerns... helping pupils consider, respond and make reasoned and informed choices relating to areas of right and wrong, moral conflict, concern for others, and the will to do what is right.	• **explore** the ways of life and application of codes of conduct of believers; • **recognise and reflect** on the difference between right and wrong, good and evil; • **develop** knowledge and understanding of why people behave in particular ways, why people adopt certain moral standpoints, and how moral decisions are made; • **reflect** on why they choose to behave in one way or another.
Social development – this concerns... helping pupils develop their sense of identity and belonging and preparing them for adult life in a plural society.	• **work** in a range of groups; • **develop** understanding of the need to live harmoniously in a plural society; • **reflect** on social issues and religious responses.
Cultural development – this concerns... fostering pupils' awareness and understanding of beliefs, practices, lifestyles and values in their own multi-cultural society and in the wider world.	• **learn** about and value the richness and diversity of cultural traditions; • **experience** music, sacred text, festivals and artistic expression from around the world; • **challenge** racism and xenophobia; • **see** the worth of themselves, their family, religion and culture.

Learning from religion

The use of the two attainment targets for RE of 'learning about religions' and 'learning from religion' is very widespread in England and Wales. In Scotland, the dimension of personal search in RME provides for a similar focus.

Aspects of RE connected with attitudes, personal beliefs and values can seem problematic, but if the focus is upon developing the pupil's skills, it immediately becomes clear that you can achieve grade A in RE as an atheist, relativist, Christian or Hindu.

So here the view that learning from religion and personal search needs to be built up in RE leads us to suggest teachers give high priority in planning to improving the reflective, engaging and responsive aspects of the subject.

Here are points to guide such developments:

All schools should give more attention to the opportunities for spiritual and moral development in RE. While most pupils are learning a great deal about religions, few are being encouraged to learn from religion (AT2).
Opportunities for reflection should be closely linked to subject content. If there is not time for pupils to reflect on the meaning of what they study, evaluate moral issues or discuss their own developing beliefs and spirituality, then either the number of religions, or the number of topics taught must be reduced. This is an issue for both schools and SACREs.

The Impact of New Agreed Syllabuses on the Teaching and Learning of RE, Ofsted, TSO, 1997,

Weave it all together	Learning about religion and learning from religion are interwoven in good RE, which combines the examination of living belief systems in the light of shared human experience to facilitate personal search.
Make space for human experience	Learning from religion makes space for all pupils to explore their own experiences, responses, beliefs and values – if RE is for all, then this matters intensely.
Start anywhere	Activities which promote learning from religion and personal reflection can be beginnings, middles or ends in a curriculum unit.
What do they think?	Many RE teachers could usefully provide more opportunities for pupils to give their own ideas, views and opinions: provide structure, time and space. No good RE happens unless pupils are challenged with this question: So what do you think?
No invasions of privacy	Keep on your toes as learning from religion can slip into invasion of privacy without care. Pupils may share very intimate ideas and feelings in good RE lessons, but this should always be by choice. Personal search work doesn't demand you wear your heart on your sleeve.
Cut the content	Even inspectors agree that too much religious content spoils learning from religion. Follow your professional judgement, and be willing to delete the section on 'theological terminology' from term one of your course. Standards of reflection and response will only rise where time and attention are given to building the necessary skills.
Design higher quality tasks	Teachers need to spend time designing excellent classroom tasks which ask autobiographical, personal, reflective and/or argumentative questions in relation to the religious material studied, and give alternatives.
Aim at the heart	RE teaching and learning needs to try to identify the core of practice and ritual in any faith: that's where learning from religion can arise. Less work on symbolic colour and more on ultimate questions is a good recipe.
Innovate boldly	Bold teaching will be willing to experiment and innovate in personal search and learning from religion.
Learning from religion is the heart of the subject	If a religiously educated young person knows seventy facts about six religions, but thinks nothing of dismissing them all casually, then RE has failed. Where pupils get the most from RE it is because they find it relevant to their own concerns and questions.

The place of learning from religion in RE

The place of learning from religion in RE is illustrated in the table below. A continuum of skills is envisaged, and the important line between processes appropriate for education and those appropriate for nurture in the context of faith is clarified. Although the diagram makes columns, there is clearly an overlap between them.

Learning about religion	Learning from religion	Spiritual and moral development in school		Nurture in faith in a religious community
Leading skills and processes:	Leading skills and processes:	Leading skills and processes:	*A clear line between appropriate aims for schools and for church, mosque or synagogue*	Leading skills and processes:
• research; • information gathering; • factual learning; • recalling information; • recording information; • developing understanding; • defining concepts; • analysis; • synthesis; • weighing up arguments.	• **reflecting on learning about religious topics;** • **asking good questions;** • **suggesting good answers;** • **responding thoughtfully to others;** • **understanding of concepts;** • **application of learning;** • **relating learning to one's own experience;** • **clarifying attitudes;** • **articulating respectful disagreements;** • **expressing responses to issues for oneself;** • **taking note of diversity in a tolerant manner;** • **accepting other views respectfully;** • **expressing personal insight in the light of religions.**	• reflection on one's own values; • responses to the attitudes of others; • clarifying and articulating beliefs; • responding to ultimate questions; • developing the determination to pursue unselfish goals; • pursuing the truth; • being tentative and at ease with diversity.		• commitment to the ideals of faith; • discernment of religious truth; • discipleship; • faithfulness to the religion; • expressing convictions; • growing in wisdom; • practising the virtues of faith; • responding to evil; • taking on the challenges of faith.

Progression

Entitlement

Pupils are entitled to a curriculum in RE through which they can make continuing progress towards achieving their potential. This requires a planned programme of study which runs through the years of education from 5 to 16, and this in turn requires co-ordination by those who write syllabus materials and those who teach them.

Planning

Planning for progression is crucial:

- between primary and secondary teachers, to enable effective transition in RE;

- between teachers within the same school.

Time for such meetings should be included in the Development Plan for RE.

Progression exemplified

In terms of quality RE, topics, themes and religions may be revisited a number of times to reinforce and develop understanding. Work needs to be progressively more challenging.

Here we have taken **two examples** which are found in most syllabuses, and have suggested how pupils might make progress.

Example one: Christians, Good Friday and Easter

	Pupils might study...	So that they might be able to...
5–6-year-olds	What use Christians make of symbols like light, the cross, the chicken and the egg on Good Friday and Easter Sunday; children's versions of the stories of Easter.	Talk about celebrating Easter and celebrating festivals in their own family or faith community; draw and write simply about eggs, new life and Easter as they make Easter cards.
9–10-year-olds	Some biblical stories of Jesus' trial, death and resurrection, through the art and music of Christians in today's church.	Design and make a symbolic 'resurrection' sculpture, window or painting, showing their learning about Christian understandings of hopes for the future.
13–14-year-olds	The place of the Eucharist and the celebration of Easter in two different Christian denominations from different countries, and the roots of these aspects of worship in the gospels; the beliefs (for example about forgiveness) which are expressed at Eucharist and Easter.	Explain some ways in which the Eucharist relates to Jesus' last supper, and the Easter festival to his resurrection; consider the significance of the Easter events for Christians, relating this to their own thinking about forgiveness, remembrance and hope.
16-year-olds	Christian doctrines of salvation from sin, and their relationship to the death and resurrection of Jesus; the teaching of another religion about the human condition.	Develop answers to questions about what Christians believe about life after death, and how this relates to the gospel accounts of the resurrection of Jesus; describe what is distinctive and what is common in Christian and other accounts of the human condition.
18-year-olds	Debates within Christianity about the historicity and theology of Easter.	Develop their own understanding of the place of Easter within the Christian faith.

Developing progression

Teachers might:

- use or adapt one of the grids on pages 67 and 68 to review the way pupils learn about a theme, a religion or a concept over a phase;

- ensure that pupils are clear about the development of their learning. Ask pupils what confuses them in RE to find out where to start!

- think through the need to keep returning to the central core concepts of RE in ways that enable pupils to make continuing progress. For example:

  - God;
  - religion;
  - worship;
  - belief;
  - sacred texts;
  - ethics.

Example two: The Qur'an – belief and practice in Islam

	Pupils might study...	So that they might be able to...
5–6-year-olds	Posters and videos showing the Qur'an and how it is used.	Recognise that the Qur'an is a special book for Muslims containing the word of Allah.
9–10-year-olds	About Muhammad ﷺ receiving the Qur'an and how this changed his life and the lives of his followers. Know how the Qur'an is used.	Know and understand that Muslims believe Muhammad to be the last prophet of Allah. That the Qur'an guides how Muslims lead their lives.
13–14-year-olds	Some sayings in the Qur'an. Discover how the Hadith may be used in relation to the Qur'an.	Understand more fully how Muslims live their lives. Compare the teachings found in the Qur'an and the Hadith with that of another faith(s) and with their own beliefs and values.
16-year-olds	The role of women and men in Islam with reference to the Qur'an.	Make informed opinions and compare with Western culture and own values.
18-year-olds	The differences within Islam with reference to the Qur'an and Islamic text.	Identify and understand the tensions and diversity within Muslim communities.

Progression in opportunities for spiritual development

RE can provide opportunities for spiritual development which are increasingly challenging and use pupils' developing skills. How far does RE enable pupils to:

- **ask and answer** questions of meaning and purpose?

- **consider** suffering and joy, hope and despair, creativity and destructiveness?

- **develop** their abilities to use stillness, silence and reflection to deepen their understanding and insight?

- **develop** their abilities to talk and listen sensitively and with empathy?

- **express** their own views, commitments, beliefs and opinions with clarity and in depth?

Examinations and RE

Examinations in Religious Studies

Teachers in secondary schools need to consider carefully the merits and disadvantages of using public examinations for RE.

Advantages

- Working towards an examination gives RE, RS or RME status in the pupil's eyes.

- Qualifications such as GCSE, Standard Grade, Highers and AS or A2 levels credit students' achievements and make them clear to the adult world and the world of work.

- National syllabuses and external assessment can make RE more rigorous.

- An RE department may strengthen its position in a school through examination success.

- Examination success at 16+ may encourage young people to study religion at higher levels, or even to become RE teachers!

Disadvantages

- National examinations may not fit well with local syllabuses, or the local needs of your pupils.

- GCSE and Standard Grade syllabuses do not cater for the full ability range, and RE needs to offer opportunities to pupils of all abilities.

- Working to an examination syllabus constrains what goes on in the RE classroom, leaving too little time for focus upon, for example, personal search.

- The educational culture of over-assessment and functionalism is less likely to be challenged from RE if the subject buys into the examination culture.

Quality RE can be found on both sides of this continuing argument.

For those who want to explore or develop their use of examinations, the questions listed on the right may help.

Qualifications for 14–16s

In Scotland, students may take Standard Grade Religious Studies. Scottish candidates may also get a qualification for a short course in Religious and Moral Education involving 40 hours of tuition.

In England and Wales, the curriculum authorities permit GCSE examinations in Religious Studies as a full course, requiring about 140 hours of tuition, or a short course, requiring about 70 hours of tuition.

There is a wide choice of subjects, religions and structures for study in all these examinations from the various awarding bodies.

Choosing an examination course: questions to consider

- Does the course match the expertise of the teaching staff?

- Does the course meet the needs of all the students bearing in mind differentiation, religious backgrounds and relevance?

- Is the assessment pattern flexible (check course-work, styles of questions in exams, and so on) so as to enable students to show what they know, understand and can do?

- Does the course enable the school to fulfil its legal obligations, for example with regard to an agreed syllabus?

- Is the course well supported by the examination awarding body, training opportunities and published resources, including broadcasts and ICT?

A rising trend

Numbers taking all these qualifications are rising currently, as part of a modest resurgence in Religious Education in the UK.

The example in the table below shows the growth of 14+ national certification in England and Wales over recent years.

England and Wales: Full and Short Course growth in GCSE RS and RE, 1987–2002

	1987	1992	1997	2002
GCSE Full Course	87,000	101,000	113,000	122,000
GCSE Short Course	-	-	12,000	201,000
Total GCSE entry	87,000	101,000	125,000	323,000

It is good to learn about faiths other than my own. I don't want to be arrogant in my faith. I like to be challenged and I consider things quite deeply in order to decide whether to apply them to my life.

16-year-old, female

Qualifications for 14–16s

A very extensive range of options for studying for national qualifications for those post-14 is available, and teachers should check them with the relevant awarding bodies. The list on the right gives a simple summary of some of the topics addressed.

Courses may focus on the belief and practice of one or two religions, or upon the religious responses to social and ethical questions and the fundamental questions of life.

Teachers should refer to the published specifications of three English awarding bodies, one in Wales and the Scottish Qualifications Authority. These have changed several times in the last few years, and may continue to be revised.

Qualifications for 16–19s

Scottish Highers and AS and A2 levels in England and Wales are available from various examining boards in Religious Studies. Again a wide variety of options is available, including a range of biblical studies, religious philosophy and ethics, the study of one from six world religions and some studies of contemporary and historical religious, social and psychological issues.

Again, numbers taking these courses have been increasing steadily in the last 10 years: around 16,000 students were working at AS level in England and Wales in 2003.

Religion and...

- environment;
- wealth and poverty;
- crime and punishment;
- medical ethics;
- the media;
- sexual ethics;
- family life;
- human equality;
- social responsibility;
- science;
- spirituality;
- the nature of belief;
- death and afterlife;
- good and evil;
- identity;
- authority and belief;
- expression in the arts;
- community;
- celebration;
- lifestyle;
- sacred texts.

Religions that may be studied

- Christianity;
- Islam;
- Hinduism;
- Buddhism;
- Sikhism;
- Judaism.

RE for all 16–19: an enriching entitlement

All students on the roll of schools in England and Wales have an entitlement to RE (unless they are withdrawn from the subject by their parents). For many school sixth forms, student indifference and hostility is reinforced in the staff room, and the entitlement is not met, leading to critical comments from inspectors.

Providing 16–19 RE for all: How?

The three main types of provision for Religious Education post-16 are:

- examination courses in Religious Studies;

- RE modules delivered within General Studies or vocational courses;

- enrichment courses – non-examination courses which are taken alongside courses leading to accreditation.

Schools may select any combination of the following types of provision:

- weekly sessions;

- modules in a cycle of enrichment studies;

- day conferences dedicated to the exploration of religious and spiritual questions.

Why?

Aside from the legal requirement, the educational rationale for RE for all 16–19 can make reference to:

- the importance of a curriculum which is broad, and encompasses the spiritual and moral as well as the work-related;

- the contributions of RE to multicultural and anti-racist education;

- the examination of ethical and religious dimensions of all other curricular subjects;

- the value of study that is mind-broadening and focused on human identity and purpose rather than the world of work;

- the inherent challenge and fascination of the study of religious and spiritual aspects of humanity.

But young people of this age-group deserve better: it is no easier to make this provision at a high level of quality than to meet other entitlements, to sex education, careers guidance, PE or Citizenship, but ignoring these enriching aspects of the curriculum impoverishes schools and students.

What can be studied?

The range of subject matter and learning styles can be very broad at this stage of education. Open-endedness, challenge and interactivity in learning are keys to success. **For example**, we have run programmes on subjects such as:

Is God?

What is the nature of claims to know or experience God? What shapes or meanings of a godless universe can be described? Do transcendent experiences imply something about God, or something about humanity? What can we learn from Sikhs and Christians about these questions?

Why evil?

What do we mean by evil, and how do we explain it? What reduces moral evils like prejudice or genocide, poverty or sexism? What insights do Buddhists, Christians and Jews have to offer?

God, ethics and sexuality

What kinds of authority in sexual morality do you reject? And accept? What makes for well being in sex ethics, and what for destructiveness? What can be learned from the study of Islamic, Humanist and Christian approaches to sex ethics?

Faith in the future

What is the future of religion, and the alternatives to religion? What stories of religious growth and decline do we find persuasive from sociology, psychology, politics and theology?

The politics of religion

What accounts of religion as repressive and liberating are to be found in our media and public life? How are film and media portraying and using religious and spiritual ideas for entertainment, politics, advertising or control?

Resourcing RE: a broad approach

What makes a good resource?

There is seldom enough money for resources in schools and teachers are ingenious in matching limited funds to unlimited needs.

This overview suggests some of the essentials or desirables for RE, and suggests that a balance between different types of resource is best for good learning.

People

The first two resources available in RE are the **teachers** and the **pupils**.

As RE is centrally concerned with shared human experience, and with a personal search for meaning, it is important that the classroom atmosphere of an RE lesson should enable pupils to feel confident about sharing their own experience, ideas and perspectives. It is appropriate that pupils should be able to bring to the enquiry the riches of their own family culture and their personal insights.

Books

The mainstay of much work in RE is the textbook. A vast range is on offer, and teachers need to use inspection copy services to agree where to invest most wisely. Whatever sections of the syllabus, or age-groups, are involved the following **four criteria** might guide the choice:

Integrity

Is it clear that the books have integrity in terms of the religions they address? For example, do books about Hinduism have consultants or authors who are Hindus?

Engagement and challenge

Are the books engaging and challenging for the age-group? For example, are the books more than merely factual, inviting engagement with issues and perspectives? Do teaching points arise from the use of good quality photographs, diagrams, drawings and other illustrations? Are these aids to understanding?

Educational standpoint

Are the books written from a clearly educational standpoint? For example, it is unsatisfactory to use books written for a church audience to teach Christianity in a mixed setting.

Value for money

Do the books represent value for money, enabling many children to learn to their potential? Some books are well worth a place in the class library, whereas others may be a basic resource for a whole year group.

Visual Resources

Video, posters, overhead transparencies, photo packs and photographs enable pupils to see for themselves aspects of the practice of religion which come from all over the world.

The internet can extend considerably the range of images which can be brought easily into the RE classroom.

Wherever an image is used (for example, activity sheet, wall display, OHT, PowerPoint presentation) it should be used as a **resource in its own right**, and not purely for decorative effect.

Responding to images

In response to an image, pupils should be asked to respond to questions such as the following:

- What do you notice?
- What is happening and who is involved?
- What do you think will happen next?
- What emotions are being shown?
- How does the image make you feel?
- What does the artist want to say?
- What questions would you like to ask the artist? How might she or he reply?
- What religious questions is this image trying to comment on?
- What have you learned from considering this image?

Artefacts

Religious artefacts in the classroom are a valuable way of adding **authenticity** and **interest** to the RE curriculum.

Collections of artefacts can be made available to schools in a variety of ways:

- school budget for RE;
- loan services (LEA or other);
- sharing between schools;
- donations from local faith communities.

However artefacts are made available, they can enrich learning when used as a window into the community which produced them. For example, a Hunger Cloth from a Christian community in the developing world can illuminate scripture, tradition and contemporary faith across the world, and stimulate pupils to reflect on the ways they might symbolise their own community life.

Visitors

Visits to school by members of a faith community are also powerful opportunities for RE. In an increasingly secular society many young people have little experience of engaging in dialogue with those who seek to live out a religious commitment.

Good practice when bringing religious visitors into school includes:

- **assessing the suitability** of a visitor for the purpose you have in mind. Ideally meet the person yourself beforehand, or seek recommendation from a reliable teacher in another school;

- **preparing well in advance** so that the visit is a natural and purposeful part of the programme of study;

- **informing parents and governors** about the nature and purpose of the visit, who the visitor is and what they represent;

- **briefing the visitor** on the ethos, aims and policies of the school, and the aspect of the RE curriculum to which they are contributing. Clarify the length and type of their input, any equipment they might need, and practicalities such as directions to the school;

- **discussing the types of teaching and learning methods** which will engage the pupils in view of their age and ability;

- **debriefing the lesson** with the visitor, so that there is opportunity to reflect on what went well, and make changes if appropriate. This is also an opportunity to say thank you.

Visits

A highlight of any RE programme is often the trip to a church, synagogue, mandir, mosque or other place of worship. This means hard work for the teacher, but the reward is that pupils have a genuine experience of the place, and the community which has created it.

Good visits have the following characteristics:

- They **build positive attitudes**;

- They are **sensitively planned**;

- They **build on preparatory work**;

- They are **interesting and active**;

- They are **integrated with a programme of study**.

A range of '**virtual visits**' can be found on the internet, and also on CD-ROM. Although these can never be as good as the 'real thing', they do have a valuable role within the RE curriculum. They can:

- **provide access** to places it is not possible to visit, for example Makkah;

- **facilitate preparation and follow-up** work for visits or visitors;

- **support research and revision**, as they can be 're-visited'.

What the pupils say

'You didn't get the "feel" of a real church.'

'A real visit would show you more and you would understand it because you've seen it.'

'You can touch it and look closely at the colours in a real church. You can't look really closely in the virtual visit.'

'You couldn't see all of the church – you can only see what they chose to put there.'

'There were no real people praying at these. It was bare.'

'It is more inspiring in a real church.'

Stories, poems and sacred texts

Providing opportunities for pupils to engage with a variety of texts important to religious traditions and faith communities is an integral part of the RE curriculum.

Select texts according to:

- the requirements of your syllabus or trust deed;
- the reading age and ability of your pupils.

Plan the use of selected texts:

- with a clear idea of learning outcomes (what do you want your pupils to know, understand and be able to do as a result of their encounter with the story or text?);
- ensuring variety of type, religion and method of presentation across a key stage;
- valuing and respecting the integrity of pupils, assuming neither a faith position nor prior knowledge.

Use a variety of ways of telling and working with religious texts or stories:

- **traditional resources** (for example, watch and listen to video and audio tapes, or use the teacher as storyteller);
- **online texts** (many sacred texts are available online, some with sound files, for example

  http://bible.gospelcom.net/bible?, www.ishwar.com or www.sacred-texts.com);
- **visitors** (invite a local member of the faith being studied into the classroom to tell the story and explain what it means to them);
- **creative writing** (for example, provide opportunities for pupils to express meaning, questions and personal reflection in the form of prose, poetry, diary entry, newspaper report, letter, script);
- **creative arts** (for example, provide opportunities for pupils to explore and express their understanding using drama, role-play, freeze-frame, dance, choral speaking, guided visualisation; cartoon drawing, art, audio and video recording);
- **reading pictures** (for example, responding to a visual representation of a story, working out what is happening in the picture and speculating about what may have happened before, and what might happen next).

CD-ROMs

Increasing access to the internet is providing teachers with a rich resource which is more up to date, dynamic and flexible than CD-ROMs can be. However, the place of the high quality CD-ROM is assured for some time to come, particularly where reasonable site or network licences are available.

As with any resource, a careful evaluation needs to be undertaken prior to purchase. The following criteria are based on guidelines provided by Becta:

Content, relevance and accuracy

- Does the list of contents match what is claimed for the resource?
- Does the content offered meet the needs of your syllabus (offering a stimulus for pupils to both learn about and learn from religion)?
- Is the information accurate, free from bias and of an acceptable moral tone?
- What is the source of the information, and what authority does this have?
- Is the balance of text, illustrations, audio and video appropriate for your pupils?

Inclusion

- Is the reading age suitable for your pupils?
- Is there an audio option, a commentary to supplement the text, or an alternative route through the information?
- Are there animation and film clips, which can help and support understanding?
- Does it offer navigation via menus, indexes or icons to support those whose spelling is weak?

Design, construction and flexibility

- Is the factual information easy to find, manipulate and retrieve?
- How interactive is the resource?
- Can the audio be switched off?
- Can text and pictures be saved to disk and/or be printed out?
- Does the copyright allow you to use the resource in the way you would like?
- Are support materials supplied?

Curriculum Online

Curriculum Online (COL) is designed to give teachers easy access to a wide range of digital learning materials which can be used to support their teaching across the curriculum. RE materials are arranged according to the QCA's non-statutory schemes of work and include the following types:

- lesson plans;
- CD-ROMs;
- interactive videos;
- simulation software;
- assessment materials;
- online services.

COL is intended to form a consistent, coherent and comprehensive online service, offering a single point of reference for teachers to find, to compare, to select and to share relevant digital resources. The COL data is searchable across a range of criteria: for example, key stage, subject, topic, free resources.

For each resource, most or all of the following information is supplied by the content provider:

- learning resource type;
- who the resource is for;
- context;
- notes for teachers;
- key stage;
- school year;
- general key words (for example Key Stage 3 RE scheme of work);
- National Curriculum key words;
- cross-curricular theme;
- inclusion theme;
- strategies keywords.

Evaluations

COL content providers can request an evaluation of their product. A fee of several hundred pounds is payable for this service. Evaluations are conducted by independent evaluators – currently Teachers Evaluating Educational Multimedia.

Not all content providers wish to, or can afford to, request an evaluation. This should be considered when consulting TEEM evaluations for RE resources. COL invites teachers to submit (online) their own reviews of resources they have purchased and used.

Teachers are encouraged to consult reviews and evaluations of COL resources for RE which are available from the sources identified on pages 75 and 78 of this *Handbook*, and which have been carried out by subject specialists. These reviews will also identify excellent resources by providers who may not (yet) be registered with COL.

Reviews and evaluations

Evaluating resources is necessary but time consuming. **Printed** and **online** reviews of RE resources reviewed by teachers, sometimes with suggestions for classroom use, are available.

Message boards for RE teachers are also helpful, as you can ask a specific question relating to your own situation.

Page 78 has details of where reviews and evaluations for ICT resources suitable for RE can be found.

Reviews

- **REtoday Reviews**
  In RE Today Services' termly subscription mailing: www.retoday.org.uk
- **The RE Site**
  www.theresite.org.uk
- **TeacherNet (QCA)**
  www.teachernet.gov.uk
- **TEEM (Teachers Evaluating Educational Multimedia)**
  www.teem.org.uk

Message boards

- **RE-XS ('Interact')**
  http://re-xs.ucsm.ac.uk
- **Yahoo!**
  http://groups.yahoo.com

Copyright

The copyright associated with all resources used in the classroom should be in line with legal requirements and LEA policy. Further information is available from:

Copyright Licensing Agency (CLA)

Information relating to text and electronic materials.
90 Tottenham Court Road, London W1T 4LP
www.cla.co.uk

Becta

Information relating to electronic materials.
Milburn Hill Road, Science Park, Coventry CV4 7JJ
www.becta.org.uk

ICT and RE

ICT in the curriculum

The ICT considerations in the National Curriculum ICT documentation support education in general and the specific aims and objectives of RE.

The National Curriculum (2000) requires that pupils be given opportunities to:

1 **apply and develop** their ICT capability through the use of ICT tools to support their learning in all subjects (with the exception of Physical Education at Key Stages 1 and 2);

2 **support their work** by being taught to:

  a find things out;

  b develop their ideas using ICT tools;

  c exchange and share information;

  d review, modify and evaluate their work.

ICT National Curriculum, page 36 (2000)

ICT skills can enable pupils to encounter religion in ways that are authentic, diverse, contemporary and global.

A teacher's entitlement

Teachers also have an entitlement to use ICT to:

* **enhance** subject expertise;

* **facilitate** planning;

* **enable** teaching to become more stimulating;

* **simplify** assessment and recording and reporting systems;

* **organise** administration;

* keep in touch with **other subject specialists and experts**.

In addition to the resources mentioned elsewhere in this section, teachers can access formal and informal professional, and subject specific, support via the selective use of **message boards** and **conferences**.

* **RE-XS ('Interact')**: http://re-xs.ucsm.ac.uk

* **BBC Religion and Ethics** site: www.bbc.co.uk/religion

* **VTC**: http://vtc.ngfl.gov.uk/docserver.php

Hardware and software

Almost all generic ICT resources can be effectively used to support teaching and learning in RE.

Hardware and software as suggested below should be included in the Development Plan for RE as a matter of course.

ICT advice can be found on Becta's website: www.ictadvice.org.uk

Essential

* **Networked computers** with a **printer**, **scanner** and **CD-ROM or DVD drive**

* **Internet** access (including **e-mail** client)

* **Word processing**, **presentation** and **data-handling** software, for example *Word*, *PowerPoint*, *Excel*, *Access* (Microsoft); *Clicker* 4 (Cricksoft)

* **Desktop Publishing** software, for example *Publisher* (Microsoft)

* **Digital stills camera**

* **Video** or **DVD**

* **CD-ROMs**

* **Data or LCD projector**

* **Electronic interactive whiteboard**

* **Concept or mind-mapping** software, for example *Kidspiration* (primary); *Inspiration* (secondary)

* **Web authoring** software, for example *FrontPage* (Microsoft); *GoLive* (Adobe) *Dreamweaver* (Macromedia)

Useful

* **Camcorder**

* **Video conferencing** access

* **Multimedia** software. for example *HyperStudio* (TAG)

Based on QCA's Guidance and Exemplification Resources 2002

When to use ICT

Effective use of ICT to support RE takes place where there is a clear understanding of when and when not to use it. The points below provide a **checklist** for any RE activity involving ICT:

ICT should be used when it:

- **supports** the achievement of RE learning objectives set by the teacher for pupils;
- **improves** the quality and enjoyment of teaching and learning;
- **adds value** to the learning process;
- **makes** planning and teaching more effective;
- **contributes** to pupils' understanding of ICT.

ICT should not be used:

- **if** learning objectives could be achieved more easily or more effectively using other resources;
- **only** and simply as a motivator;
- **where** the ICT detracts from the RE being taught;
- **where** there is no opportunity for reflection on its use.

> Using ICT in RE: Supporting a pupil's entitlement
> *(Becta/QCA, June 2000)*

Authentic task-setting

Effective use of ICT as a tool to support RE requires **challenging** and **authentic** task-setting. Michelle Selinger writes:

'Research on the benefits of setting authentic tasks to pupils has been shown to increase motivation and improve learning.'

She then defines authentic tasks as:

- 'tasks which pupils can relate to their own experience inside and outside of school;
- tasks which an experienced practitioner would undertake.'

In RE this would mean setting tasks which engage pupils from any background in profound spiritual issues for themselves, through an encounter with religious material.

> *¹Michelle Selinger, in* Issues in teaching using ICT, *edited by Marilyn Leask (2001), ISBN 0-415-23867-6*

ICT in the RE classroom

Whether the teacher has access to a single computer or a multimedia suite, there many ways in which ICT can support the RE curriculum. ICT can be used 'hands on' in the lesson, or the results of ICT use can be brought into the classroom, for example stimulus material (by the teacher) or the results of research (by pupils in homework).

Some uses of ICT in RE

The internet enables:

- access to online documents from different religious traditions, archives of newspapers from around the world and current religious information and events;
- 'visiting' places otherwise inaccessible;
- access to online message boards and conferences for pupils and teachers.

CD-ROMs enable:

- access to a vast range of data;
- illustration of unfamiliar or sensitive situations and events.

Electronic whiteboards support:

- whole-class teaching, including use of concept mapping software to aid visual thinking and *PowerPoint* presentations to support learning;
- 'walk-throughs' of CD-ROMs, software and tasks prior to a lesson.

Digital cameras provide:

- an immediate opportunity to record classroom activity;
- facility for pupils to manipulate images in class, for example adding speech bubbles to record understanding or reflection and as a record of pupil progress.

E-mail and video conferencing enable:

- engagement in dialogue and collaboration with individuals or groups within and outside the UK;
- access to key people, for example an author, religious leader, university lecturer.

Talking word processors support:

- pupils' learning in reading and writing.

Assessment issues

The guidelines for assessment are broadly the same for all tasks, including those which involve ICT. However, it will also be helpful if the teacher can ensure that:

- assessment is based on the RE objectives of the task set;

- assessed tasks have been well focused and designed to enable pupils to demonstrate their learning;

- pupils have the appropriate ICT skills they need to complete the RE task;

- pupils understand the purpose of the ICT task and how they will be assessed against the objective;

- there is clear guidance on how the source of material from CD-ROM or website should be acknowledged in pupils' work;

- collaborative work has an element of peer- and/or self-assessment.

Evaluating websites

Any resource brought into the classroom needs evaluation; websites are no exception. The internet is non-judgemental, unregulated, unauthorised and unbalanced, which means teachers need to take extra care with the evaluative process.

Many points are the same as for evaluating a CD-ROM (see page 74); however, it is worth asking questions like the following about the **authority and credibility of the author**:

- Is the **author** identified?

- Does that author have some **authority** on the subject? How do you know?

- Is the **material screened**? By whom? Why?

- Are **sources attributed** and **dated**?

- Is **evidence cited**?

- Are there regular **updates** and **new pages**?

- Are any **discussions moderated**? By whom?

- Is content **objective or subjective**?

- Does it promote **acceptable views** (for example, on race)?

The internet as a resource

The vast number of websites which have the potential to support RE can be accessed through a small number of **gateway sites**.

There are also useful links given in the increasing number of sites which aim to support **study and revision**.

Ready-made reviews of a wide range of ICT resources are available, as are **exemplification materials** for RE, including the use of ICT.

Gateway sites

- **The RE Site**
  http://resite.org.uk

- **RE Exchange Service (RE-XS)**
  http://re-xs.ucsm.ac.uk

- **BBC Religion and Ethics**
  www.bbc.co.uk/religion

Study support and revision

- **The GCSE RE Site**
  http://re-xs.ucsm.ac.uk/gcsere

- **BBC Bitesize Revision**
  www.bbc.co.uk/schools/gcsebitesize

- **REsauce**
  www.resauce.org

- **RS Web** (AS/2 Level)
  www.rsweb.org.uk

Reviews of websites and ICT resources

- **REtoday Reviews**
  In RE Today Services' termly subscription mailing: www.retoday.org.uk

- **TeacherNet**
  www.teachernet.gov.uk

- **The RE Site**
  www.theresite.org.uk

Guidance and exemplification materials

- **Virtual Teacher Centre**
  http://vtc.ngfl.gov.uk

- **National Curriculum in Action**
  www.ncaction.org.uk/subjects/re

- **Your own Grid for Learning**

Appendix: Collective worship

Current legislation

Current legislation seeks to ensure the broadly Christian basis of collective worship but without undervaluing the rich contribution other faiths can make.

Some argue that providing a daily act of quality collective worship is a burden schools are not equipped for and periodically there are calls to change legislation or at least to re-assess Circular 1/94 (Guidance on RE and collective worship).

Collective worship can be of immense value as it seeks to:

- **promote and develop** the common values underpinning the life of the school;

- **contribute to opportunities** for the spiritual , moral, social and cultural development of pupils, including providing 'space' for those who wish to worship God (however defined or understood);

- **provide opportunities for pupils** (and staff) to share, celebrate, and express their beliefs, and to reflect together.

Three guiding principles

1 **Collective worship should be inclusive.** It should:

- **be pupil-centred** – related to their own experience, relevant to their concerns and shaped to their needs;

- **acknowledge diversity and affirm** those present, whatever their faith or non-faith background – it should respect the integrity of pupils and teachers;

- **involve** those present as active participants;

> *Collective worship ... does not have the sole responsibility for pupils' SMSC development ... but it provides opportunities to make values explicit, to challenge pupils' thinking, extend their emotional repertoire and celebrate who they are and what the school community stands for. Above all it must offer a unique opportunity for reflection and, for those for whom it is appropriate, a time for worship.*
>
> Collective Worship in the Primary School,
> *Julie Grove & Louise Tellam, 2001, Solihull MBC*

- **foster** a sense of community – a sense of shared values, identity, outlook, ethos and purpose.

2 **Collective worship should be educational.** It should:

- **be a learning experience** of real quality, properly planned, prepared, executed and evaluated;

- **be properly resourced** – time, training, books, music, and so on;

- **be related to the school's aims** for collective worship and be consonant with the ethos and general educational aims of the school;

- **offer a variety** of experiences;

- **celebrate** the successes and **share** the disappointments of the school community;

- **be open** – broadening and deepening knowledge and understanding of the issues being focused upon.

3 **Collective worship should be spiritual.** It should:

- **provide a 'breathing space'** in the busy whirl of school activity, a time to gather, be still and reflect, a time to refresh the spirit;

- **provide opportunities** for pupils to consider questions and responses to belief in God;

- **provide an atmosphere** conducive to allowing worship to take place – music, a visual focus, an appropriate setting all helping to create this special atmosphere;

- **provide opportunities** for reflection on the significance of the spiritual dimension to their own and other people's lives – through, for example, listening to music, responding to the arts, hearing from others, listening to words from the sacred writings of different traditions, prayer and meditation:

- **be open enough** for pupils to respond to the spiritual dimension, while accepting that some pupils will make no personal response.

A process for developing collective worship in your school...

1 Where are we now?

Take an honest look at present practice – strengths and areas in need of development.

- What do staff and pupils think about their experience of collective worship?
- What resources and expertise have you to draw upon?

2 Where do we need to be?

Overall a school should be:

- implementing legal requirements;
- developing educational potential;
- delivering quality experience.

All of this contributes to the provision of opportunities for the spiritual, moral, social and cultural development of pupils.

Depending on where the school is when it starts the process, there may be other specific aspects which need developing.

3 What do we need to make it happen?

Planned priorities need to be established in order to move forward – a realistic timescale is necessary and account should be taken of resource implications (time and talents, as well as financial).

Needs will vary but could include:

- writing a school policy;
- INSET;
- additional resources;
- drawing in more people (staff, pupils and visitors);
- developing cross-curricular links;
- increasing staff confidence;
- developing a more positive attitude;
- a focus on forward planning and record keeping.

Collective worship should contain times of quiet reflection, which enable pupils to develop the deepest values and aspirations of the human spirit (for example, love, peace, wonder, imagination, sensitivity, integrity).

Space for Reflection, edited by Lesley Beadle, RE Today Services, 2002

4 How are we going to know when we've got there?

Thought should be given to identifying success criteria at the start and these will depend on the focus given. Some are relatively easy – 'We had no policy before; now we do'.

The effectiveness of such a policy document is harder to assess, though pupils' responses provide a lot of information.

5 When are we going to review?

Reviewing the collective worship programme regularly (every 3 years, say) as part of the school development plan will be beneficial. This helps in planning a realistic timescale for development and prepares for beginning the cycle again.

An A–Z of themes for collective worship...

Achievement   Beginnings   Change
Discipleship   Experience   Forgiveness
Good and evil   Happiness
Imagination   Journeys
Key people   Life and death
Messengers   Neighbours
Optimism and hope
Quality of life   Parables
Rights and responsibilities
Science and religion
Universe   Treasures
Wisdom   Voices
Youth   Xanadu   Zeal

CHESTER COLLEGE WARRINGTON LIBRARY

REtoday Services   *A Teacher's Handbook of Religious Education*